WORLD WAR II FOR TEENS – 21 SECRET OPERATIONS

Daring, Dangerous, and Often Unseen Missions
That Changed the Course of History

James Burrows

© **Copyright 2024 - All rights reserved.**

The content contained within this book may not be reproduced, duplicated or transmitted without direct written permission from the author or the publisher.

Under no circumstances will any blame or legal responsibility be held against the publisher, or author, for any damages, reparation, or monetary loss due to the information contained within this book, either directly or indirectly.

Legal Notice:

This book is copyright protected. It is only for personal use. You cannot amend, distribute, sell, use, quote or paraphrase any part, or the content within this book, without the consent of the author or publisher.

Disclaimer Notice:

Please note the information contained within this document is for educational and entertainment purposes only. All effort has been executed to present accurate, up to date, reliable, complete information. No warranties of any kind are declared or implied. Readers acknowledge that the author is not engaged in the rendering of legal, financial, medical or professional advice. The content within this book has been derived from various sources. Please consult a licensed professional before attempting any techniques outlined in this book.

By reading this document, the reader agrees that under no circumstances is the author responsible for any losses, direct or indirect, that are incurred as a result of the use of the information contained within this document, including, but not limited to, errors, omissions, or inaccuracies.

Other Books by James Burrows

What You Need To Know:

World War I for Teens
World War I for Kids
World War II for Teens
World War II for Kids
World War II for Teens – 21 Secret Missions
The Vietnam War for Teens

The Ultimate Guide:

Egyptian Mythology for Kids
Greek Mythology for Kids
Norse Mythology for Kids

Other Books:

The Art of War – Sun Tzu
Mediations – Marcus Aurelius

CONTENTS

THE HIDDEN WAR

1. OPERATION GREEN ROOM (1941): THE SAS' FIRST TRIUMPH

2. OPERATION CHARIOT (1942): THE DARING RAID ON SAINT-NAZAIRE

3. OPERATION ANTHROPOID (1942)

4. OPERATION FRANKTON (1942): THE COCKLESHELL HEROES

5. OPERATION MUSKETOON (1942): COMMANDO RAID ON GLOMFJORD POWER SATION, NORWAY

6. OPERATION BITING (1942): CAPTURING GERMAN RADAR TECHNOLOGY TO SHIFT THE BALANCE IN THE AIR WAR

7. OPERATION GUNNERSIDE (1943): SABOTAGING NAZI GERMANY'S ATOMIC AMBITIONS

8. OPERATION MINCEMEAT (1943): DECEIVING THE ENEMY AND CHANGING THE COURSE OF THE WAR

9. OPERATION CROSSBOW (1943): THE FIGHT AGAINST HITLER'S VENGEANCE WEAPONS

10. OPERATION CHASTISE (1943) – THE DAMBUSTERS RAID

11. OPERATION JAYWICK (1943): ATTACK ON JAPANESE SHIPPING

12. OPERATION FORTITUDE (1944): THE MASTERSTROKE OF DECEPTION

13. OPERATION JEDBURGH (1944): A CRUCIAL LINK IN THE D-DAY STRATEGY

14. OPERATION SUNRISE (1945): SECRET NEGOTIATIONS THAT HASTENED THE END OF WORLD WAR II

15. OPERATION PASTORIUS (1942): A FAILED GERMAN SABOTAGE MISSION ON U.S. SOIL

16. OPERATION GREIF (1944): A TALE OF DECEPTION AND CHAOS

17. OPERATION BERNHARD: THE NAZI PLAN TO FORGE CHAOS

18. OPERATION VALKYRIE (1944): THE ATTEMPT TO END HITLER'S REIGN

19. OPERATION WILLI (1940): THE PLOT TO KIDNAP A PRINCE

20. OPERATION PAPERCLIP (1945): RECRUITING THE BRAINS BEHIND NAZI GERMANY'S TECHNOLOGY

21. THE MANHATTAN PROJECT: CREATING A WEAPON THAT CHANGED THE WORLD

THE LEGACY OF COURAGE AND INNOVATION

ABOUT THE AUTHOR

THE HIDDEN WAR

Imagine being in the middle of the most dangerous war in history and realizing that sometimes, winning isn't about fighting harder - it's about outsmarting your enemy. Welcome to the fascinating world of World War II undercover operations and deceptions, where plans were hatched in secret, double agents weaved webs of lies, and entire armies were created out of thin air to fool the Nazis. Where missions often operated on a razor's edge, their success or failure hinging on quick thinking, courage, and sometimes sheer luck.

This is the world of secret missions: daring plots, deception, covert operations, and behind-the-scenes heroics that were every bit as dangerous, and pivotal to the outcome of the war, as the battles raging across the front lines.

This was the war you don't always hear about - the one fought in whispers and shadows. It wasn't just about brute force; it was about trickery, creativity, and pulling off stunts so bold that they sound like something out of a Hollywood movie.

Take Operation Fortitude, for example. The Allies wanted to convince Hitler that the D-Day invasion was coming to a completely different place, so they built fake armies, used dummy tanks and planes, and even planted false intelligence. And it worked! Hitler kept his forces in the wrong location, giving the Allies the upper hand when they landed in Normandy.

But that's just one example. This book dives into a world where spies turned traitors into allies, where secret radio messages carried life-or-death plans, and where deception wasn't just a strategy - it was an art. These undercover operations saved thousands of lives, shortened the war, and made some of the greatest victories possible.

Why does this matter? Because it reminds us of the power of human ingenuity. These weren't just military geniuses and secret agents; they were ordinary people using extraordinary creativity to outthink one of the most formidable war machines in history.

So, get ready to explore the thrilling stories behind the operations that changed the course of World War II. From fake invasions to double agents and daring lies, you'll see how the Allies turned deception into a weapon of war. The best part? These stories aren't just brilliant - they're true. Prepare to step into the hidden war where brains beat brawn, and the stakes were as high as they get.

The Purpose and Premise of Covert Operations

Covert operations during WWII were not merely an add-on to conventional battles; they were instruments of deception, innovation, and resilience that often dictated the outcomes of larger campaigns. These operations reflected a deeper understanding of warfare as a multidimensional endeavor, where controlling information, spreading misinformation, and crippling an enemy's resources could prove as decisive as firepower.

For the Allies, secret operations became a lifeline, particularly in the face of a well-prepared and resourceful Axis. The Allied powers recognized that they could not rely solely on brute strength. They needed ingenuity, misdirection, and collaboration with underground movements to weaken the Axis powers from within. These operations also highlighted the collaborative efforts between nations, as intelligence agencies like Britain's MI6, America's Office of Strategic Services (OSS), and resistance groups across occupied Europe united against the Axis.

Both sides of the war were involved in covert operations. For instance Nazi Germany, ran operations like Pastorius, aimed at sabotaging the U.S., or Bernhard, an ambitious counterfeiting plan to destabilize Allied economies.

The Global Context of WWII and the Need for Secrecy

World War II was a global conflict like no other. With nations spanning six continents embroiled in the war, it became a clash of ideologies, economies, and technological innovation. The scale of the conflict necessitated secrecy, as open warfare alone could not address the complexities of a war fought across diverse terrains and cultures.

The Axis powers, led by Germany, Japan, and Italy, had established formidable military forces, and their rapid conquests left much of Europe and the Pacific under their control by 1942. For the Allies, overcoming these odds required a strategy that could outthink, outmaneuver, and outwit the enemy. This need for ingenuity led to an era of covert operations where deception and subterfuge took center stage.

Secrecy was also vital in this era of limited communication technologies. Secure transmission of information was an enormous challenge, as radio waves could be intercepted, codes broken, and couriers captured. This drove the creation of groundbreaking encryption methods, such as the Enigma machine used by the Germans and subsequently decoded by the British, which provided the Allies with a treasure trove of intelligence.

Key Themes of the Hidden War

The hidden war revolved around several interwoven themes that defined its scope and impact:

Intelligence Gathering

Intelligence agencies became the lifeblood of covert operations. From deciphering enemy codes to gathering information on troop movements, intelligence was the cornerstone of strategic decision-making. For example, the British cryptanalysis teams at Bletchley Park cracked the Enigma code, providing the Allies with critical insights into German plans. Similarly, resistance movements across occupied Europe relayed invaluable information about Axis logistics and fortifications.

Sabotage

Sabotage missions aimed to disrupt the enemy's infrastructure, supply chains, and war capabilities. Operations like Gunnerside, which targeted Nazi Germany's heavy water production facility in Norway, exemplify how precision sabotage could cripple Axis ambitions, such as the development of nuclear weapons.

Deception

Deception operations were masterpieces of psychological warfare, designed to mislead the enemy and create confusion. Operation Fortitude, for instance, successfully diverted German attention away from Normandy in the lead-up to D-Day, making it one of the most significant deception campaigns of the war.

Special Forces

The war saw the emergence of specialized units trained for covert missions. Britain's Special Operations Executive (SOE), America's OSS, and resistance groups across Europe carried out missions that ranged from blowing up bridges to assassinating high-ranking officials. These teams operated in hostile environments, relying on stealth, cunning, and adaptability.

Psychological Warfare

Beyond physical sabotage and deception, psychological tactics sought to undermine the morale of enemy troops and civilians. Leaflet drops, false broadcasts, and exaggerated reports of Allied strength were all used to sow fear, doubt, and confusion within Axis ranks.

Stories of Daring and Ingenuity

Covert operations were not only ingenious but also deeply human, filled with tales of extraordinary bravery, sacrifice, and creativity. One of the most audacious examples of psychological and operational ingenuity was Operation Mincemeat. In this operation, British intelligence created a fictitious identity for a corpse and planted misleading documents suggesting that the Allies planned to invade Greece rather than Sicily. The Germans fell for the ruse, diverting their forces and enabling a successful Allied landing in Sicily.

Even the skies were a battleground for covert operations. Operation Chastise, famously known as the Dambusters Raid, involved precision bombing of German dams. The successful breach of the dams not only caused massive flooding but also disrupted German industry and morale.

The Dual Nature of Covert Operations

While the Allied operations are often celebrated, it is important to recognize that the Axis powers also engaged in covert tactics. Operation Pastorius, for example, involved German saboteurs landing on U.S. shores with plans to disrupt industries and infrastructure.

Germany's Operation Bernhard attempted to destabilize the Allied economies by flooding them with counterfeit currency. Though it did not achieve its intended scale, the operation showed the Axis's creativity in pursuing non-conventional warfare.

These operations highlight the duality of covert missions, where both sides sought to outwit each other in a deadly game of strategy and counter-strategy.

The Legacy of the Hidden War

The legacy of the hidden war extends beyond the immediate outcomes of WWII. The tactics and strategies developed during these missions laid the groundwork for modern espionage, special forces, and intelligence operations. Organizations like the CIA and MI6 owe much of their methodology to the pioneering efforts of WWII operatives.

Moreover, the stories of bravery, resilience, and ingenuity continue to inspire. They remind us that wars are not won by brute force alone but by the courage to take risks, think creatively, and act decisively. The hidden war reveals a side of WWII that is less visible yet no less impactful - a war where success depended not on the size of an army but on the power of an idea and the determination of a few!

❖ *DID YOU KNOW*

Look out for incredible war facts throughout the book, some amazing, some weird, some horrible and some just mind-boggling!

Let's jump in and uncover some of these exciting, secret operations!

N GREEN ROOM (1941): THE SAS' FIRST

Let's start our journey with the original special forces unit, the British SAS. The establishment of the Special Air Service (SAS) in 1941 marked a pivotal moment in the history of British military operations. This elite commando unit was conceived by the audacious David Stirling, who envisioned small, elite units capable of bold and fearless operations behind enemy lines. They used the desert's vastness to their advantage, avoiding detection while striking critical Axis infrastructure.

Lieutenant-Colonel Sir David Stirling, founder of the SAS. He was nicknamed "The Phantom Major" by Erwin Rommel, because of his elusiveness and hit-and-run tactics.

❖ *DID YOU KNOW*

- Some members of the British military through the SAS as operating 'unfairly', and their means of fighting were not 'honorable'!

What Was Happening in The War at This Point

By late 1941, the North African campaign had become a critical theater in World War II. British and Commonwealth forces were engaged in a bitter struggle against the Afrika Korps, commanded by the brilliant German general Erwin Rommel. The harsh desert environment presented unique challenges, making logistics, mobility, and air support crucial for both sides.

The Allies launched Operation Crusader in November 1941, a large-scale offensive to relieve the besieged garrison at Tobruk and push Axis forces out of Cyrenaica (eastern Libya). However, Axis air superiority posed a significant threat to the operation's success. The SAS was tasked with undermining this superiority by targeting Axis airfields along the Libyan coast.

During the North African Campaign of World War II, the German and Italian forces under the command of Field Marshal Erwin Rommel (the "Desert Fox") were primarily focused on conventional warfare strategies, involving large-scale tank battles and controlling key supply routes. Their defensive planning often overlooked unconventional threats, such as the highly mobile and innovative tactics of the British Special Air Service (SAS).

Heavily armed SAS patrol, North Africa

Objective

Operation Green Room, undertaken in December 1941, would become the SAS's first notable success, redeeming the unit after its initial failure in Operation Squatter. This mission not only established the SAS as a formidable force but also provided a blueprint for future special forces operations.

The primary objective of Operation Green Room was to disrupt German and Italian airpower in North Africa during the Allied campaign by destroying as many enemy aircraft as possible. This was to be accomplished through covert assaults on Axis airfields, a task requiring precision, stealth, and meticulous coordination.

The operation aimed to achieve several goals:

- Cripple Axis air capabilities, giving the Allies an advantage in aerial dominance.

- Undermine enemy morale by demonstrating the vulnerability of their positions.

- Establish the SAS as an effective and indispensable asset in the Allied strategy.

This mission followed the disastrous Operation Squatter, the SAS's first combat mission, which had ended in failure. The mission saw the SAS parachuting behind enemy lines in Libya in November 1941 to destroy enemy aircraft and support Operation Crusader. However, it was launched into a severe storm, one of the worst the region had seen in 30 years. The SAS troops were dispersed over a wide area, and only 21 of the 55 men who took part returned. One of the aircraft carrying the troops was shot down, killing all 15 soldiers and the crew. Operation Green Room was an opportunity to redeem the fledgling unit and prove its worth.

SAS troops jumping from scaffolding while undergoing parachute training at Kabrit, Egypt

One of the key advantages the SAS had was the element of surprise. The Germans didn't expect any attacks from the desert for a number of reasons:

1. **Perceived Impassability of the Desert**
   The vast, harsh deserts of North Africa were considered natural barriers. The Germans believed that no significant force could navigate these extreme terrains without established supply lines.

2. **Focus on Strategic Points**
   German and Italian forces concentrated on defending ports, airfields, and key towns along the Mediterranean coastline, from where they thought any attacks would originate. The interior desert was seen as a logistical challenge with limited strategic value.

3. **Underestimation of Allied Innovation**
   The Axis forces were unfamiliar with the long-range, hit-and-run tactics used by the SAS and other Allied units like the Long Range Desert Group (LRDG). The SAS leveraged their deep knowledge of the desert and used it to bypass German defenses.

Details

Planning the Mission

After the failure of Operation Squatter, David Stirling and his men reevaluated their tactics. They decided to forgo parachute drops, which had proven unreliable, and instead partnered with the Long Range Desert Group (LRDG), a reconnaissance and raiding unit adept at navigating the vast desert terrain. The LRDG provided the SAS with transport and logistical support, enabling them to reach their targets by truck rather than by air.

The target was four Axis airfields near the Libyan coast. These airfields housed dozens of German and Italian aircraft, which were critical to Axis operations in North Africa. The plan involved infiltrating the airfields at night, planting time-delayed explosives on the aircraft, and retreating before the bombs detonated.

The Execution

In December 1941, a group of 65 SAS soldiers set out on their mission. Traveling in trucks provided by the LRDG, they navigated the harsh desert environment over 3 days, to reach their targets. The operation required absolute silence and precision to avoid detection by enemy forces.

Upon reaching the airfields, the SAS operatives stealthily approached the aircraft. Using time-delayed explosive charges, they rigged each plane to detonate after the team had safely withdrawn. Despite the high stakes, the mission unfolded with remarkable efficiency.

SAS operatives relied on surprise and aggression. One soldier famously smashed the cockpit of a plane with his bare hands when they ran out of explosives.

The team withdrew under the cover of darkness, avoiding pursuit and returning to their base without suffering a single casualty.

The Outcome

Operation Green Room was a resounding success. The SAS destroyed 61 enemy aircraft across four airfields, significantly reducing Axis airpower in the region. This achievement boosted the morale of Allied forces and demonstrated the value of the SAS's unconventional tactics.

Significance of Operation Green Room

The destruction of 61 Axis aircraft disrupted enemy operations and provided the Allies with a much-needed reprieve from aerial bombardments. This allowed the Allied forces to regain momentum in the North African campaign and contributed to the eventual success of Operation Crusader.

The operation marked the SAS's transition from a fledgling experiment to a proven combat unit. The mission demonstrated the effectiveness of small, highly trained teams operating behind enemy lines and set the stage for future special forces operations.

The success of Operation Green Room influenced the development of special forces units worldwide. The mission highlighted the importance of adaptability, meticulous planning, and collaboration with other units, such as the LRDG.

The audacity of the operation sent a powerful message to the Axis powers. Even Field Marshal Erwin Rommel, known as the "Desert Fox," reportedly expressed admiration for the SAS's effectiveness.

❖ DID YOU KNOW

- The SAS's motto is "Who Dares Wins," embodying the spirit of Operation Green Room. The mission's daring nature set the tone for the unit's future operations.

- The SAS's effectiveness drew the ire of the Nazis. Hitler's Commando Order, issued in 1942, declared that captured SAS operatives were to be summarily executed, reflecting the fear and hatred the unit inspired among Axis forces.

- By the end of the African campaign, the SAS had destroyed more than 400 enemy planes on the ground.

- Winston Churchill was a huge supporter of the SAS. In fact, his son Randolph joined an SAS mission in May 1942, to plant explosives in the harbor of the Italian-occupied port of Benghazi.

Legacy of Operation Green Room

Operation Green Room was a turning point for the SAS, cementing its place as one of the most effective special forces units in history. The operation's success was not merely a tactical victory; it was a statement of intent, showcasing the power of unconventional warfare in a conflict dominated by traditional strategies.

For the men who participated, it was a triumph born of resilience, ingenuity, and sheer audacity.

From humble beginnings, the SAS emerged as a symbol of daring and excellence, a legacy that began with the flames and explosions of Operation Green Room.

Unrelated to the Green Room operation, but an interesting example of the incredible bravery and resilience of SAS soldiers, let's take a quick look at Corporal T Sillito. He was a member of a four-man SAS patrol tasked to blow up the rail line in the enemy's rear, just before the offensive at El Alamein. After a firefight with the enemy, Sillito got separated from the rest of his group, and set out to walk the 100 miles, across the desert, back to the British lines, without food or water, a gruelling week-long experience which he only just survived. The photograph taken below is after several days in hospital following his rescue, with his feet still bandaged.

Corporal T Sillito

2. OPERATION CHARIOT (1942): THE DARING RAID ON SAINT-NAZAIRE

World War II saw countless acts of heroism and strategic ingenuity, but few operations matched the sheer audacity and precision of Operation Chariot.

On the night of March 28, 1942, British forces launched a daring raid on the French port of Saint-Nazaire to cripple Germany's naval dominance. This covert operation combined deception, bravery, and meticulous planning to achieve a singular goal: rendering the massive Normandie dry dock unusable, thus limiting the reach of the formidable German battleship Tirpitz.

What Was Happening in The War at This Point

By early 1942, the Allied war effort was fraught with challenges. Germany had solidified its hold on much of Europe, and the Kriegsmarine (German Navy) was a potent force. The Tirpitz, sister ship of the infamous Bismarck, loomed as a psychological and tactical menace. Though largely inactive, its mere presence in Norwegian fjords forced the Allies to allocate significant resources to counter its threat.

Meanwhile, the French coastline, under German occupation, bristled with defenses. Ports like Saint-Nazaire became vital hubs for Nazi logistics, repair, and resupply operations. The Allies recognized the strategic importance of disrupting these operations to level the playing field at sea.

Operation Chariot was conceived as a bold strike to deliver a significant blow to German naval capabilities, demonstrating Allied ingenuity and determination to disrupt enemy plans, no matter the cost.

Objective

The primary objective of Operation Chariot was straightforward but critical: destroy the Normandie dry dock in Saint-Nazaire. At the time, this facility was the only dry dock on the Atlantic coast capable of accommodating the mighty Tirpitz, a battleship that posed a significant threat to Allied convoys. By eliminating this strategic asset, the Allies aimed to prevent Tirpitz from entering the Atlantic, where it could wreak havoc on shipping lanes vital to the war effort.

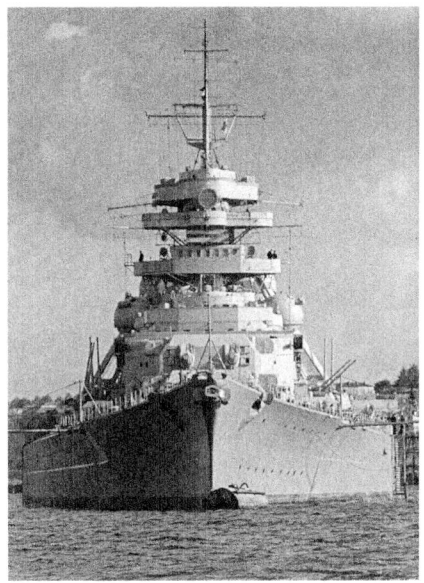

German battleship, Tirpitz

The dry dock's destruction would force German capital ships to return to home ports in Germany for repairs, where they would be at risk of sinking from Royal Naval ships in the English Channel or the North Sea.

Details

The plan for Operation Chariot centered on the use of an old British destroyer, HMS Campbeltown, modified to serve as an explosive-laden battering ram. With 4.5 tons of high explosives concealed in her hull, the Campbeltown was to be rammed into the Normandie dry dock gates, delivering a devastating delayed-action explosion. A flotilla of smaller motor launches and motor torpedo boats would accompany the destroyer, delivering commandos tasked with targeting other key installations in the port.

Preparations and Departure

The mission involved 612 men, including 265 commandos and 345 sailors. The HMS Campbeltown was disguised to resemble a German destroyer by altering her silhouette and flying a German naval ensign. To maintain the element of surprise, the operation relied on a nighttime approach and strict radio silence.

Motor launch (ML) of the type which took part in the raid on St Nazaire. Sixteen such MLs were assigned to the force and were to carry commandos and demolition parties into St Nazaire. Their frail wooden hulls offered scant protection and only three of the craft survived the operation.

On the night of March 26, 1942, the task force set sail from Falmouth, England, under the command of Commander Robert Ryder and Lieutenant Colonel Augustus Charles Newman, the operation's naval and commando leaders, respectively.

Execution of the Raid

As the flotilla approached Saint-Nazaire under the cover of darkness, they faced intense enemy fire from shore batteries. Despite sustaining heavy damage, HMS Campbeltown pressed on, ramming into the dry dock gates with precision at 1:34 AM. The commandos disembarked and began their assault, targeting power stations, pump houses, and other infrastructure vital to the dock's operation.

Fighting raged throughout the port as the commandos engaged in fierce close-quarters combat with German defenders. Although vastly outnumbered, the raiders inflicted significant damage before attempting to withdraw.

The Explosion and Aftermath

As planned, the explosives aboard HMS Campbeltown detonated at noon on March 28, obliterating the dry dock gates and flooding the facility. The blast killed approximately 360 German personnel and caused extensive damage to the surrounding area.

HMS Campbeltown was essentially a Trojan horse. Its delayed-action explosives were timed to detonate hours after the attack, ensuring maximum confusion among German personnel. Some Germans had even boarded the ship out of curiosity before the explosion.

Of the original task force of 612, only 228 men managed to return to England. 169 were killed in action, while 215, mostly wounded, were captured and spent the remainder of the war in German POW camps.

Significance of Operation Chariot

Operation Chariot was a resounding tactical success. The destruction of the Normandie dry dock effectively removed Saint-Nazaire from the German naval equation for the rest of the war. Without the dry dock, the Tirpitz was unable to operate in the Atlantic, allowing the Allies to redirect resources to other critical fronts.

Despite the high cost in lives, the raid boosted Allied morale, demonstrating that even the most fortified Nazi positions could be breached with ingenuity and determination.

❖ *DID YOU KNOW*

- To divert attention, a decoy fleet transmitted fake radio signals, simulating a large-scale naval attack elsewhere. This ruse successfully drew German forces away from Saint-Nazaire, contributing to the raid's success.

- Commandos fought with incredible bravery despite overwhelming odds. One group of 100, led by Lieutenant Colonel Newman, held out for hours after their escape route was cut off, refusing to surrender until their ammunition was exhausted.

- The raid resulted in the award of 89 decorations for valor, including five Victoria Crosses - the highest military honor in the British armed forces. These awards underscored the extraordinary bravery displayed during the operation.

- A handful of commandos managed to evade capture by trekking over 60 miles through German-occupied France before being rescued by resistance fighters and smuggled to safety.

- French civilians working at the port played a subtle but significant role, aiding the commandos where possible and sabotaging German efforts to repair the dry dock in the aftermath of the raid.

- The Tirpitz never entered the Atlantic, instead remaining in Norwegian fjords until she was destroyed by the RAF in Operation Catechism on November 12, 1944.

Shell from the Tirpitz, fired in 1944 and found unexploded in Ullsfjord, Norway.

- The operation has been called 'The greatest raid of all time', for its daring and almost suicidal concept.

Legacy of Operation Chariot

Operation Chariot's impact reverberated far beyond the war itself. It set a precedent for future commando operations, highlighting the value of small, highly trained units capable of striking critical targets. Its success also bolstered Allied morale, serving as a beacon of hope during one of the darkest periods of the war.

In the post-war years, Saint-Nazaire became a symbol of resistance and resilience. Today, memorials and museums honor the memory of those who participated in this extraordinary raid, ensuring that their bravery and sacrifice are never forgotten.

3. OPERATION ANTHROPOID (1942)

Up next is Operation Anthropoid, a daring and highly strategic mission aimed at assassinating Reinhard Heydrich, one of Adolf Hitler's most trusted and ruthless officials.

Heydrich, often referred to as 'The Butcher of Prague' and 'The Architect of the Holocaust', was the Reich Protector of Bohemia and Moravia and a key figure in orchestrating the Nazi regime's genocidal policies. The mission, carried out by Czech and Slovak operatives trained by the British Special Operations Executive (SOE), sought to eliminate Heydrich to deal a psychological and operational blow to the Nazi leadership and inspire resistance within occupied Czechoslovakia.

What Was Happening in The War at This Point

By 1942, World War II had reached a critical and tumultuous phase. Nazi Germany controlled vast swathes of Europe, including Czechoslovakia, which had been occupied since 1939. The German grip on the region was brutal, with resistance movements crushed under severe reprisals. Reinhard Heydrich, sent by Hitler to solidify control over the area, became infamous for his brutal suppression of dissent and his role in implementing the "Final Solution" to exterminate European Jews.

Objective

Heydrich's power extended beyond Czechoslovakia. As head of the Reich Main Security Office (RSHA) and a leading architect of the Holocaust, he played a central role in shaping Nazi terror policies across occupied Europe. The Allied forces, recognizing his importance and influence, saw an opportunity to strike at the Nazi hierarchy by targeting Heydrich. For the exiled Czechoslovak government in London, assassinating Heydrich was not just a military objective - it was a way to assert their relevance, inspire resistance, and demonstrate to their citizens that Nazi oppression could be resisted.

Reinhard Heydrich

Details

Planning and Training

Operation Anthropoid was meticulously planned by the Czechoslovak government-in-exile, working closely with the British SOE. Josef Gabčík and Jan Kubiš, two young resistance fighters, were selected for the mission. They were flown into Czechoslovakia in December 1941 as part of a larger parachute drop, along with operatives for other missions.

Gabčík and Kubiš underwent intense training in sabotage, hand-to-hand combat, and covert operations. The decision to assassinate Heydrich in broad daylight within Nazi-controlled Prague was bold and fraught with risks, reflecting the high stakes of the mission.

Jan Kubiš (left) and Jozef Gabčík (right)

The Ambush

On May 27, 1942, Gabčík and Kubiš carried out the ambush on Heydrich as he traveled in his open-top Mercedes-Benz near a curve in the road in the Prague suburb of Libeň. Gabčík attempted to fire his Sten gun at Heydrich but the weapon jammed. Thinking the attack had failed, Heydrich ordered his driver to stop the car and confront the attackers.

Reinhard Heydrich's car after the assassination attempt

At that moment, Kubiš threw an anti-tank grenade, which exploded near the car, wounding Heydrich severely with shrapnel in his abdomen and back. Both operatives managed to escape the scene despite sustaining minor injuries. Heydrich was rushed to the hospital and initially seemed to be recovering. However, he died on June 4, 1942, due to septicemia caused by his wounds.

The Aftermath - Nazi Reprisals

The assassination of Heydrich enraged Hitler and the Nazi leadership, triggering a wave of brutal reprisals across Czechoslovakia, with an estimated 5,000 people being murdered by the Nazis, and 13,000 arrested. Entire villages were wiped out in retaliation. The village of Lidice was razed to the ground, its male population executed, and its women and children sent to concentration camps. Ležáky, another village, met a similar fate. These massacres were intended to deter further resistance but instead galvanized anti-Nazi sentiment.

The Fate of the Operatives

Gabčík, Kubiš, and their collaborators initially evaded capture. However, they were betrayed by a fellow resistance member, leading the Nazis to corner them in the Church of Saints Cyril and Methodius in Prague. After a fierce firefight on June 18, 1942, both men took their own lives rather than be captured. Their bravery and sacrifice became a symbol of resistance against tyranny.

Significance of Operation Anthropoid

The assassination of Reinhard Heydrich dealt a significant psychological blow to the Nazi leadership. Heydrich's death deprived the regime of one of its most capable and feared officials, disrupting Nazi operations in Czechoslovakia and beyond. For the resistance movements in Europe, the operation was a beacon of hope, demonstrating that even the most ruthless Nazi leaders were not invincible.

Heydrich's death created a temporary leadership vacuum in the Nazi administration of Bohemia and Moravia, hampering their ability to suppress resistance and implement policies effectively. Although the Nazis retaliated brutally, their overreaction alienated the local population and strengthened the resolve of resistance fighters.

Operation Anthropoid inspired resistance movements across occupied Europe by showing that even high-ranking Nazis could be targeted successfully. The bravery of Gabčík and Kubiš became legendary, and their story was a rallying cry for freedom fighters.

The operation served as a propaganda victory for the Allies, demonstrating their commitment to fighting Nazi oppression and supporting resistance movements in occupied countries. It also strengthened the credibility of the Czechoslovak government-in-exile, bolstering their position on the international stage.

❖ *DID YOU KNOW*

- Reinhard Heydrich's confidence in his own invincibility played a role in his downfall. Despite warnings about potential assassination attempts, he insisted on traveling in an open-top car without significant security. This arrogance made him an easier target for Gabčík and Kubiš.

- The success of Operation Anthropoid depended heavily on the underground resistance network in Prague, which provided shelter, intelligence, and logistical support to Gabčík and Kubiš. Without these courageous individuals, the mission would not have been possible.

- Operation Anthropoid was the only successful government-organized assassination of a top-ranking Nazi official.

- The operatives were betrayed by a member of the resistance, Karel Čurda, who revealed their hiding place in exchange for a reward from the Nazis. His actions led to the deaths of the operatives and several innocent civilians. Čurda was later executed for his betrayal after the war.

- The Lidice massacre was one of the most horrific reprisals in World War II. After the war, Lidice was rebuilt nearby, with the original site preserved as a memorial, and its story became a powerful reminder of Nazi atrocities and the courage of those who resisted them.

Legacy of Operation Anthropoid

Operation Anthropoid stands as one of the most audacious and impactful resistance operations of World War II. The assassination of Reinhard Heydrich was a bold strike at the heart of the Nazi leadership, demonstrating the courage and determination of the Czechoslovak resistance and their Allies. While the operation came at a heavy cost, including brutal reprisals and the loss of many innocent lives, it served as a turning point in the fight against Nazi oppression.

Gabčík and Kubiš, along with the countless others who supported them, left a legacy of heroism. Their sacrifice highlighted the importance of resistance, the power of collaboration between nations, and the enduring fight for freedom against tyranny. Operation Anthropoid was not just a mission to eliminate a Nazi leader - it was a symbol of defiance and hope in the darkest days of the war.

4. OPERATION FRANKTON (1942): THE COCKLESHELL HEROES

Let's take a look at Operation Frankton, one of the most audacious and innovative sabotage missions of World War II.

Conducted by British Royal Marine Commandos, this daring raid targeted German shipping in the port of Bordeaux, France. Using miniature 'cockleshell' canoes, the operation combined ingenuity, bravery, and endurance, leaving a lasting legacy in the history of special operations.

What Was Happening in The War at This Point

By 1942, German-controlled ports in France were crucial for maintaining the Nazi war machine. Bordeaux, located 70 miles inland along the Gironde River, was particularly significant, as it served as a transit point for materials vital to the Axis powers.

Objective

The primary objective of Operation Frankton was to cripple German merchant shipping in the heavily defended port of Bordeaux, a vital hub for Nazi supply lines. By planting limpet mines on ships, the mission aimed to disrupt the flow of supplies critical to Germany's war effort, particularly goods being transported to and from Japan and occupied Europe.

Traditional bombing raids on Bordeaux had proved too risky and ineffective due to strong anti-aircraft defenses and the strategic location of the port. The British Combined Operations Headquarters, under Lord Mountbatten, devised a radical alternative: a stealth mission using small, easily concealable canoes to penetrate the port's defenses and carry out the sabotage.

The operation was a testament to the British military's creativity during a time of desperate need for victories against Nazi Germany.

Details

Planning and Preparation

Operation Frankton was the brainchild of Major Herbert "Blondie" Hasler, a Royal Marine known for his innovative thinking. Hasler believed that small, highly mobile teams could accomplish what larger forces could not: penetrate heavily defended areas and strike with precision.

The Cockleshell Canoes

The mission utilized specially designed collapsible canoes nicknamed 'cockleshells.' These lightweight, two-man vessels were portable yet sturdy enough to navigate the treacherous Gironde River.

Operation Frankton at the launch of the attack

The Team

The operation comprised 12 Royal Marine Commandos divided into six canoe teams.

Each canoe was outfitted with limpet mines, rations, and equipment for long-distance paddling.

Training

The team underwent rigorous training in paddling, navigation, and sabotage techniques. They practiced under conditions simulating the Gironde River's currents and prepared for the physical and psychological challenges of the mission.

Insertion: December 7, 1942

The commandos were deployed from the submarine HMS Tuna, which surfaced off the French coast. Under cover of darkness, the six canoes were launched into the Atlantic, beginning their perilous journey toward Bordeaux.

Navigating the Gironde River

The team paddled 70 miles up the Gironde River over four nights, avoiding detection by German patrols and navigating strong currents, freezing temperatures, and darkness.

To maintain stealth, the commandos concealed their canoes during daylight hours, hiding in reeds and using camouflage to blend into the riverbanks.

Sabotage in Bordeaux

On the night of December 11–12, 1942, the remaining teams reached the port of Bordeaux.

They attached limpet mines to the hulls of six German merchant ships. The mines were timed to detonate after the commandos had escaped, ensuring maximum damage while minimizing their exposure to danger.

The Escape

The mission was only partially successful in terms of personnel. Out of the six canoes launched, only two reached Bordeaux. Four teams were either intercepted or lost to the river's harsh conditions.

After the sabotage, Major Hasler and Marine Bill Sparks embarked on an arduous journey to escape. With the help of the French Resistance, they trekked over 100 miles across occupied France, eventually reaching Spain after two and a half months. From there, they were smuggled to Gibraltar and returned to the UK.

Challenges and Risks

- ***Hostile Environment:*** The Gironde River was heavily patrolled by German forces, with searchlights and armed boats monitoring the waterways. Any misstep would mean certain death or capture.

- ***Harsh Conditions:*** The winter of 1942 was particularly cold, and the commandos faced freezing temperatures and rough waters. Exposure to the elements caused several team members to succumb to hypothermia and exhaustion.

- ***Unrelenting Pressure:*** The psychological toll of constant vigilance, the threat of discovery, and the grueling physical effort required to paddle long distances took a significant toll on the commandos.

The Outcome

Operation Frankton was a remarkable success in terms of its primary objective. The limpets, attached to the hulls of German ships, caused significant damage to the vessels in Bordeaux. This disrupted vital shipping operations, particularly the transportation of raw materials critical for the German war machine.

Impact on the War Effort

The operation delayed the transport of essential supplies to Germany, forcing the Nazis to divert resources to repair and defend their shipping infrastructure.

British Prime Minister Winston Churchill praised Operation Frankton as one of the most daring raids of the war.

Significance of Operation Frankton

While the human cost was high, the mission achieved its goal of disrupting German shipping. It demonstrated that small, well-trained teams could achieve significant results with minimal resources.

❖ *DID YOU KNOW*

- Major Hasler and Bill Sparks survived on minimal rations during their escape, often scavenging for food and relying on the generosity of French civilians.

- The commandos carried cyanide capsules in case of capture, knowing the Gestapo would subject them to brutal interrogation.

- The cockleshell canoes were so small and silent that they could pass within feet of enemy patrols without detection.

- Only two of the 10 men who launched from the submarine survived the raid. Of the other eight, six were executed by the Germans and two died from hypothermia.

- Winston Churchill is reported to have said that Operation Frankton shortened the war by six months, a testament to its strategic significance.

Legacy of the Cockleshell Heroes

The mission inspired the development of similar sabotage and infiltration operations.

Major Hasler and Bill Sparks became celebrated figures, with their story immortalized in books, documentaries, and the 1955 film The Cockleshell Heroes. They were commemorated with a statue in Bordeaux, honoring their bravery and the impact of their mission.

Operation Frankton monument, Montalivet-les-Bains (Gironde, France)

Operation Frankton was a bold and imaginative mission that showcased the ingenuity, courage, and resilience of the British Royal Marines. Despite overwhelming odds and immense risks, the Cockleshell Heroes succeeded in striking a critical blow against the German war machine.

Their story is one of extraordinary heroism and sacrifice, a testament to the power of determination and innovation in the face of adversity.

5. OPERATION MUSKETOON (1942): COMMANDO RAID ON GLOMFJORD POWER SATION, NORWAY

We now move to Norway and the first of 2 secret operations we'll look at the country, that tragically ended in murder for the participants, at the hands of the German SS.

Operation Musketoon, conducted in September 1942, was a daring commando raid by the British on the Glomfjord power station in Norway – an equalling daring raid to that of Operation Gunnerside later in the war. The mission was to sabotage the plant, which supplied electricity to a crucial aluminum smelter and other industries that were vital to the German war effort, especially the production of aircraft. The operation was carried out by a team of 12 men, including British commandos led by Captain Graeme Black, and Norwegian operatives from the Special Operations Executive (SOE).

Glomfjord's hydroelectric power plant in Norway

Details

The team was transported covertly via the Free French submarine Junon from the

Orkney Islands, across the North Sea to Norway. Once on land, they embarked on a difficult three-day march across mountains and glaciers to reach their target. They spent a further 3 days gather intelligence about the target, before they launched a night-time attack on the power station, being careful to evacuate the Norwegian workers.

One team targeted the turbine hall and five huge generators which they destroyed. The other team had set explosives, with 30-minute fuses, on huge 7 feet diameter pipes, feeding water to the plant.

The Outcome

The explosives caused significant damage - from high up on the mountain the pipes ruptured and millions of gallons of water, and tons of mud and rocks fell on the plant.

The operation was a success, and although the plant wasn't completely destroyed, it was put out of action for a number of months, long enough for the Germans to decide to end their expansion programme.

The Escape

The escape proved disastrous. One of the operatives, Corporal Erling Djupdraet, was mortally wounded. 4 of the team managed to escape to Sweden, and eventually back to Britain.

The remaining commandoes were captured by German forces, and taken to the infamous Colditz Castle prison camp where they were interrogated.

Colditz Castle POW prison

Hitler's Commando Order

In 1942, enraged by commando raids in Dieppe and the SAS in North Africa, Hitler issued his Commando Order. Issued on October 18, 1942, and classified 'MOST SECRET' – all copies were supposed to be memorized and destroyed – it decreed that 'German troops will exterminate' British commandos or special forces personnel in Nazi-controlled territory, 'without mercy wherever they find them... they are to be exterminated to the last man... If such men appear to be about to surrender, no quarter should be given to them.'

The captured commandoes from Operation Musketoon, were the first to be executed under the Commando Order. They were sent to Sachsenhausen Concentration Camp, near Berlin, where all seven men were executed by a bullet in the back of neck, on October 23, 1942 – they were Graeme Black, Joe Houghton, Miller Smith, Cyril Abram, Eric Curtis, Bill Chudley and Reg Makeham.

The execution of British and other allied soldiers in uniform, following their surrender, was a war crime. There were apparently additional instructions that the murders would be kept secret, the bodies buried in unmarked graves, and the fate of the captured commandos would not be revealed to the Red Cross or anyone else.

The Commando Order was illegal, and recognised as such by the Nuremburg trials. German officers were convicted of war crimes for carrying it out. While some German officers, most notably Rommel, ignored the order, others carried it out with great enthusiasm.

6. OPERATION BITING (1942): CAPTURING GERMAN RADAR TECHNOLOGY TO SHIFT THE BALANCE IN THE AIR WAR

Time for an operation that was not an attack on the enemy, but an effort to gain intelligence.

Operation Biting was a daring British commando raid with a critical objective: to seize components of the German Würzburg radar system at a facility in Bruneval, France. This mission aimed to provide the Allies with vital intelligence about the German air defense network, enabling the development of countermeasures to mitigate the Luftwaffe's effectiveness against Allied bombing raids.

What Was Happening in The War at This Point

By 1942, air supremacy had become a decisive factor in World War II. The British Royal Air Force (RAF) relied heavily on strategic bombing campaigns to weaken Germany's industrial and military capabilities. However, these efforts faced a formidable obstacle: the Germans' advanced radar systems, such as the Würzburg radar, which allowed them to detect incoming Allied aircraft and coordinate Luftwaffe fighter intercepts with devastating precision.

Objective

The Würzburg radar was a groundbreaking piece of technology, capable of tracking aircraft up to 40 miles away. Its role in Germany's integrated air defense network made it a top priority for Allied intelligence. British scientists and military strategists recognized that understanding this radar system could pave the way for improved countermeasures, such as radar jamming and more effective bombing tactics.

Würzburg mobile radar

When British intelligence discovered a Würzburg radar installation on the French coast at Bruneval, they devised an ambitious plan to capture the radar and bring it back to Britain for analysis. This bold operation would combine precise military execution with the element of surprise.

Men of 'C' Company, 2nd Parachute Battalion, arriving in Portsmouth after the Bruneval raid, February 28, 1942.

Details

Planning the Mission

Operation Biting was meticulously planned and executed by a specialized unit of British commandos, supported by the Royal Air Force (RAF) and Royal Navy. The raiding party was drawn from the newly formed 6th Airborne Division, particularly No. 2 Commando, and included technical experts capable of dismantling and securing the radar equipment.

The operation involved three critical phases:

- Infiltration: The commandos would land near the radar site via parachute, ensuring a stealthy approach.

- Assault: The team would storm the radar station, neutralize German defenders, and dismantle the Würzburg radar.

- Extraction: The commandos, along with the captured radar components, would retreat to the coast and escape via naval vessels.

The Night of the Raid

In the early hours of February 28, 1942, British paratroopers took off from airfields in England and crossed the English Channel. As they neared Bruneval, the men parachuted into position under cover of darkness. Their precise landing near the radar site was a testament to the skill of both the pilots and the paratroopers.

The raid itself unfolded with remarkable efficiency:

- **Surprise Attack:** The commandos launched a swift and coordinated assault on the radar station. Despite facing resistance from the German defenders, they quickly overpowered them, capturing key components of the radar system intact.

- **Technical Expertise:** Specialists in the raiding party dismantled the radar equipment with impressive speed, prioritizing components that would provide the most valuable intelligence.

- **Capture of German Personnel:** Several German technicians were taken prisoner, offering a potential treasure trove of information about radar operations and German defensive strategies.

The Outcome

Once the radar components were secured, the commandos retreated to the coast, where Royal Navy motor torpedo boats awaited them. The extraction phase was not without challenges, as the raiders came under fire from German reinforcements alerted by the commotion. However, the majority of the team managed to escape with their precious cargo.

Operation Biting Memorial located at Bruneval, France

Significance of Operation Biting

The success of Operation Biting had far-reaching consequences for the Allied war effort.

It revolutionized radar countermeasures. The captured Würzburg radar components were transported to Britain and analyzed by top scientists, including experts from Bletchley Park, the center of Allied codebreaking efforts. This analysis revealed critical insights into the radar's operating principles, allowing the Allies to develop effective countermeasures such as radar jamming technology. These advancements significantly improved the RAF's ability to evade German air defenses during bombing missions.

Operation Biting was a morale-boosting victory at a time when the war's outcome was far from certain. It demonstrated the ingenuity and bravery of British forces, showcasing their ability to strike deep into German-occupied territory and achieve strategic objectives.

The raid set a precedent for future airborne operations, highlighting the effectiveness of paratroopers in executing high-risk missions behind enemy lines. This success contributed to the growing prominence of airborne divisions in subsequent campaigns, such as D-Day and the glider assault on Pegasus Bridge.

The raid's success highlighted vulnerabilities in German defenses, undermining their aura of invincibility. The loss of the Würzburg radar at Bruneval was both a practical and symbolic setback for the Nazis.

❖ DID YOU KNOW

- The raiders' night-time parachute landing was an incredible feat of precision. Despite the challenges of navigating in darkness and enemy territory, the commandos landed close enough to their target to execute the operation seamlessly.

- The operation was designed to look like a simple commando raid to prevent the Germans from realizing their radar technology was compromised.

- British scientists dismantled and reverse-engineered the Würzburg radar with astonishing speed. Within weeks, they had developed countermeasures that would prove pivotal in future air campaigns.

- French Resistance fighters provided critical intelligence about the radar site's layout and German troop movements, underscoring the vital role of local collaborators in Allied operations.

- The success of Operation Biting foreshadowed the large-scale airborne operations that would become a hallmark of Allied strategy later in the war, including the Normandy landings in 1944.

- Despite the raid's high-stakes nature, British casualties were relatively light. Most of the raiding party returned safely, a testament to the operation's meticulous planning and execution.

- The Germans had believed the Bruneval radar site was too well-defended to be attacked. The raid shattered this illusion, forcing them to reassess the security of their installations.

Legacy of Operation Biting

Operation Biting was a resounding success, achieving its objective and yielding intelligence that shifted the balance in the air war. By capturing and studying the Würzburg radar, the Allies gained a technological edge that undermined the effectiveness of Germany's air defense network. The raid also demonstrated the potential of airborne forces, paving the way for more ambitious operations in the years to come.

Operation Biting was a critical turning point in World War II's battle for technological supremacy. Its success not only bolstered the Allied air campaign but also demonstrated the value of precision raids in gathering intelligence and undermining enemy capabilities. It was a daring mission, carried out by a small group of highly trained and courageous individuals.

7. OPERATION GUNNERSIDE (1943): SABOTAGING NAZI GERMANY'S ATOMIC AMBITIONS

Back to Norway for our 2nd operation in that country, and another mission to destroy an industrial plant. This operation is especially memorable for the incredible feats of survival of those involved, surviving in brutal and extreme conditions.

During World War II, the Allied forces feared the catastrophic potential of Nazi Germany developing an atomic bomb. Central to this concern was the German-controlled heavy water plant at Vemork, Norway. Heavy water (deuterium oxide) was a key component in nuclear research, and the Vemork plant was the only facility in Europe producing it in significant quantities. To cripple Nazi nuclear ambitions, the Allies launched a daring sabotage mission: Operation Gunnerside.

Preceding this effort was Operation Grouse, an essential preparatory mission marked by resilience and survival in one of the harshest environments on Earth. Together, these operations became legendary for their strategic importance, audacity, and heroism.

Operation Grouse: The Prelude to Freshman and Gunnerside

Objective

The operation was run from October 1942 – February 1943 to establish a base of operations, gather intelligence about the plant's defenses, and prepare for the larger sabotage mission. They successfully set up the groundwork and made contact with local resistance groups.

The Team

Operation Grouse was conducted by four Norwegian commandos: Jens-Anton Poulsson (team leader), Arne Kjelstrup, Knut Haugland, and Claus Helberg. Trained by the British Special Operations Executive (SOE), these men were handpicked for their endurance, survival skills, and local knowledge.

HM King Haakon VII of Norway with (from the left) Knut Haukelid, Joachim Rønneberg, Jens Anton Poulsson (shaking hands with the King)

The Challenge

The commandos parachuted into the remote Hardangervidda plateau, a frozen and treacherous wilderness in southern Norway. This region, one of Europe's most inhospitable, presented extraordinary survival challenges.

Extreme Survival

Dropped with limited supplies and equipment, the Grouse team faced brutal winter conditions. Temperatures plummeted below freezing, and the plateau was blanketed with snow. With resupply missions delayed, the team survived for weeks on minimal rations, including moss, roots, lichen, and the occasional reindeer they hunted. Despite the hardships, the team maintained their focus on the mission, scouting the area and preparing for the arrival of reinforcements.

Amazing Fact

The Grouse team consumed raw moss and boiled lichen to stay alive. The local Sami people taught them survival techniques, including methods for hunting reindeer in the frigid tundra.

Operation Freshman (November 1942)

Operation Freshman was the sabotage mission that Grouse was supporting. It 39 British engineers and RAF personnel who were sent in by 2 gliders to destroy the plant itself. Unfortunately, the operation was unsuccessful due to poor weather conditions, navigational errors, and the difficulty of the terrain. One of the gliders crashed into a mountain, killing everyone on board. The other crash-landed far from the intended destination. Some of the soldiers on board died in the crash, and the survivors were rounded up and executed by the Gestapo.

Operation Freshman memorial at the site of Skitten Airfield

The Wait

After the failure of Operation Freshman, the Grouse stayed in the field, enduring months of isolation, extreme cold, and malnutrition in the depths of the Norwegian winter. Communication with the SOE was sporadic due to radio issues and the long Norwegian nights. Despite these obstacles, the Grouse team never wavered, exemplifying resilience and determination.

Operation Gunnerside (February 1943): Sabotage at Vemork

Operation Gunnerside consisted of six Norwegian commandos led by Joachim Rønneberg. The team also included Knut Haukelid and Hans Storhaug. This group was trained in sabotage tactics by the SOE and parachuted into Norway to join the Grouse team, taking 5 days of trekking in blizzards to meet up.

The objective was to destroy the Vemork heavy water plant to prevent Germany from advancing its nuclear weapons program.

Vemork Hydroelectric Plant at Rjukan, Norway in 1935. In the front building, the Norsk Hydro hydrogen production plant.

What Was Happening in The War at This Point

By early 1943, the Allies realized the critical importance of disrupting German nuclear research. Intelligence suggested that Germany was accumulating heavy water for experiments that could lead to an atomic bomb. Operation Gunnerside was devised as a follow-up to Operation Grouse, leveraging the groundwork laid by Poulsson's team.

Details

The Attack

Once the Gunnerside team linked up with the Grouse commandos, they devised a meticulous plan to infiltrate the heavily guarded Vemork plant.

Approach Through The Gorge

To reach their target, the team had 3 options: walk through a minefield, cross a bridge guarded by Germans, or scale a 500 foot cliff. To avoid detection, the commandos chose the most difficult route: descending into the steep gorge below the plant, crossing a frozen river, and climbing the rocky slopes to the facility. The treacherous terrain and freezing temperatures added immense difficulty to the mission.

Infiltration

On the night of February 27, 1943, the team cut through a security fence and entered the plant undetected. Using forged identity cards and wearing civilian clothing, they avoided arousing suspicion.

Sabotage

The commandos planted explosives on critical machinery used in the production of heavy water. To maximize the operation's impact, they used delayed fuses to ensure the team's safe escape – however, at the last minute, Ronneborg shortened the fuses from 2 minutes to just 30 seconds – he wanted to hear the explosions as they escaped!

Outcome

The explosion destroyed key equipment and heavy water stocks. However, it only made the plant inoperable for a few months. By May 1943, the heavy water production facilities were rebuilt and operating again.

Escape and Survival

After completing the sabotage, the team split into small groups to evade capture. Despite Nazi efforts to hunt them down, the commandos used their knowledge of the Norwegian wilderness to remain undetected and all 9 escaped to safety.

Most team members trekked across snow-covered terrain for days. Several skied over 200 miles to reach neutral Sweden. Their physical endurance and resourcefulness were vital to their survival in the extreme environment.

The Nazis deployed 12,000 troops sweeping the Vemork area looking for the saboteurs forces and conducting reprisals in the region, but the commandos' familiarity with the terrain and their ability to blend in with locals thwarted all efforts to apprehend them.

Significance of Operation Gunnerside

The operation was hailed as one of the most successful sabotage missions of World War II. It significantly delayed German progress in nuclear research and showcased the effectiveness of Allied special operations.

The destruction of the Vemork plant hindered Germany's ability to produce heavy water. Combined with later bombing raids by the Allies, it ensured that the Nazis could not pursue an atomic bomb.

The operation boosted the morale of resistance movements across Europe, proving that strategic sabotage could thwart even the most formidable enemy plans.

After the Gunnerside operation, the building at Vemork was still safely standing, so in November 1943, American bombers dropped 700 bombs on the plant. Although the bombing still did not destroy the plant, the Germans decided to move their supplies to Germany. Germany's attempt to move their heavy water supplies from Norway to Germany also ended in failure at the hands of Norwegian saboteurs. Led by Knut

Haukelid, a group of Norwegian saboteurs was ordered to sink a ferry carrying the Germans' semi-finished heavy water products to research centers in Germany. On February 20, 1944, the "Hydro" ferry was sunk by an explosion in the boat's bow, and the Germans lost their last supplies of heavy water from the Vemork plant.

❖ DID YOU KNOW

- Rønneberg and his group crossed the border into Sweden using skis, carrying only minimal supplies. Their journey through harsh blizzards remains one of the most remarkable escapes of the war.

- The operation was celebrated in a 1965 film called 'The Heroes of Telemark' starring Kirk Douglas.

- The commandos all dressed in British uniforms underneath their snowsuits. They thought that if the British were blamed for the sabotage rather than the Norwegian resistance, the local population would be less likely to face German repercussions.

- Hitler's standing order was that all commandos captured by German troops would be interrogated and killed without remorse. Before the Gunnerside mission began, the Norwegian commander handed out suicide capsules to the men involved.

- Norwegian Royal Army Colonel Leif Tronstad reportedly told the commandos, "I cannot tell you why this mission is so important, but if you succeed, it will live in Norway's memory for a hundred years."

Legacy of Operation Gunnerside

The resilience of the Grouse and Gunnerside teams inspired future generations of special forces. Their survival under extreme conditions, tactical brilliance, and unwavering commitment to their mission became legendary.

The actual impact of Grouse, Freshman, and Gunnerside on the outcome of the war and on the German atomic bomb programme remains difficult to assess. We now know that Germany was actually a long way from being able to produce a nuclear weapon. But the allies didn't know this. And these operations were truly the most daring conducted in Norway.

8. OPERATION MINCEMEAT (1943): DECEIVING THE ENEMY AND CHANGING THE COURSE OF THE WAR

Now it's time for one of the strangest operations of WW2. This one involves a corpse that fooled Hitler, and helped to change the course of World War II!

The primary goal of Operation Mincemeat was to mislead the Axis powers, particularly Nazi Germany, into believing that the Allied forces planned to invade Greece and Sardinia instead of Sicily. This strategic deception aimed to divert German troops away from Sicily, ensuring a smoother and more successful Allied invasion of the island.

What Was Happening in The War at This Point

By 1943, the tide of World War II had begun to turn against the Axis powers. The Allies were preparing to launch an invasion of southern Europe to weaken German control and establish a foothold for further offensives. Sicily was a crucial target, as its capture would provide a strategic gateway to Italy and the European mainland. However, the island's importance made it an obvious choice for invasion, and the Germans had fortified their defenses in anticipation.

To overcome this challenge, British intelligence recognized the necessity of deception. The Germans had to be convinced that the invasion would target a different location. The Allies needed to create a credible ruse to manipulate German strategy - and so, Operation Mincemeat was born.

The operation was part of a broader deception strategy known as Operation Barclay, which was a designed to make the Nazis think the Allies would invade the Balkans, diverting attention and resources from the true Allied objectives.

Details

Operation Mincemeat was one of the most audacious and meticulously planned acts of deception in modern warfare. It was conceived by two British intelligence officers, Ewen Montagu and Charles Cholmondeley, who devised an elaborate plan to plant false intelligence in enemy hands.

Charles Cholmondeley and Ewen Montagu, two of the British intelligence officers involved in the planning of Operation Mincemeat, shown in front of the vehicle transporting the body of Glyndwr Michael for pick up by submarine.

The Creation of Major William Martin

Central to the plan was the creation of a fictitious British Royal Marine officer, "Major William Martin." This non-existent officer was to serve as the unwitting courier of fake invasion plans. To make the ruse believable, British operatives obtained the body of a deceased homeless man, Glyndwr Michael, who had died from ingesting rat poison. The body was chosen carefully to ensure it matched the physical characteristics expected of a military officer.

The corpse was dressed in a British officer's uniform and equipped with carefully constructed personal items, including photographs of a fictitious fiancée, a love letter, and theater ticket stubs. These details were intended to make "Major Martin" appear as a real, fully fleshed-out individual.

Photograph of fictitious fiancée, an MI5 staff member

The Fake Documents

The pièce de résistance of the operation was a set of forged documents carried in a briefcase chained to the corpse's wrist. One letter that was called 'the Vital Document' was a letter from General Sir Archibald Nye, Vice Chief of the Imperial Defense Committee, to General Harold Alexander, the highest ranking British general in North Africa, addresses increasing forces for the upcoming (false) attack on Greece and Crete, and the use of an invasion of Sicily (the true attack) as a diversion to fool the Germans into not reinforcing Greece.

Delivery to the Germans

The body of "Major Martin" was placed inside a sealed canister, placed aboard a submarine in Scotland and then released off the coast of Spain near Huelva, a region known for its pro-German sympathies. The submarine crew was told the canister contained a secret meteorological device. It was made to look as if the Major Martin had been killed in a plane crash. British intelligence relied on the likelihood that the Spanish authorities, who recovered the body, would share the documents with German agents operating in the area.

HMS Seraph

The German Response

As anticipated, the documents were passed on to German intelligence. The Germans believed the ruse and diverted significant forces to Greece and Sardinia, leaving Sicily relatively under-defended.

On May 14, 1943, in a meeting with Admiral Karl Doenitz, Adolf Hitler declared that Sicily was not the next landing and that Greece and Sardinia must be reinforced. Hitler ordered the 1st Panzer Division moved from France to Greece along with 7 infantry divisions from Italy, and an additional 10 infantry divisions from Italy to the Balkans. Sardinia was also heavily reinforced with aircraft and naval elements as well. Even when the invasion of Sicily began on July 9, 1943, Hitler apparently still believed a major attack would fall on Greece.

Significance of Operation Mincemeat

Operation Mincemeat was a resounding success and is often hailed as one of the most effective wartime deceptions in history. The operation directly contributed to the Allied forces' ability to launch a successful invasion of Sicily, known as Operation Husky, on July 9, 1943. With German and Italian forces distracted and stretched thin, the Allies encountered far less resistance than they would have otherwise.

The capture of Sicily marked a turning point in the war, paving the way for the Allied invasion of Italy and eventually leading to the collapse of Mussolini's regime. Operation Mincemeat not only demonstrated the power of psychological warfare but also showcased the ingenuity and creativity of British intelligence.

❖ *DID YOU KNOW*

- The operation's codename, "Mincemeat," was part of a standard list of co-denames chosen at random. However, given the grim nature of the mission - using a corpse to deceive the enemy - it turned out to be eerily fitting.

- The British intelligence team went to extraordinary lengths to make the ruse believable. For instance, the forged letters contained references to fictitious operations that aligned with known Allied strategies. Even the uniform buttons on "Major Martin's" clothing were checked to ensure they were regulation-issue.

- The operation relied on Spain's nominal neutrality during the war. While Spain was officially neutral, it had sympathies for the Axis powers, making it the perfect intermediary for passing along the fake documents to German agents.

- British domestic intelligence agency MI5 played a key role in ensuring that details about Operation Mincemeat remained secret. The operation was so sensitive that very few people within the Allied command were aware of its existence.

- After the war, the details of Operation Mincemeat remained classified for many years. It wasn't until the 1950s that Ewen Montagu published a book titled The Man Who Never Was, revealing the true story behind the operation.

- The story of Glyndwr Michael, the man whose body was used for the mission, is both tragic and heroic. A homeless man who died under desperate circumstances, his unwitting contribution to the war effort became a pivotal moment in history. It was not until 1997 that Major Martin's real identity was revealed when the Commonwealth War Graves Commission added Glyndwr Michael's name to the grave in Huelva.

- One of the most astonishing outcomes was how easily the Germans accepted the deception. Hitler's belief in the fake documents demonstrates the power of carefully crafted misinformation.

- Ian Fleming, the creator of James Bond, worked in Naval Intelligence in WW2, He produced a list of various schemes to deceive the Germans and number 28 on the list was the idea of letting the Germans discover a corpse with a set of false plans on it!

Legacy of Operation Mincemeat

The operation was a masterstroke of deception that exemplified the ingenuity and resourcefulness of Allied intelligence during World War II. By convincing the Germans to focus their defenses on Greece and Sardinia, the operation directly facilitated the successful invasion of Sicily and marked a turning point in the Allies' campaign in Europe. It remains one of the most remarkable stories of wartime espionage, demonstrating that battles are not only won with weapons but also with wit and strategy.

9. OPERATION CROSSBOW (1943): THE FIGHT AGAINST HITLER'S VENGEANCE WEAPONS

Next, we explore an operation to reduce the impact of German rockets that were terrorizing London.

World War II saw the rise of innovative and devastating weaponry, but few threats loomed as ominously as the German V-1 and V-2 rockets. Known as "revenge weapons," these missiles were designed to strike fear into the hearts of the Allies by raining destruction upon British cities. In response, the Allies launched Operation Crossbow, a coordinated effort combining intelligence, espionage, and precision bombing raids to neutralize the rocket threat at its source. This campaign was a race against time, pitting Allied forces against one of Nazi Germany's most advanced technological achievements.

What Was Happening in The War at This Point

By 1943, the tide of the war was beginning to turn against Germany. The Allies were advancing in North Africa, planning the invasion of Italy, and preparing for the eventual assault on mainland Europe. However, Hitler's secret weapons program posed a new and terrifying challenge.

The V-1, nicknamed the "buzz bomb" for its distinctive sound, was the world's first cruise missile. It was followed by the V-2, a revolutionary ballistic missile capable of striking its target faster than the speed of sound. These weapons were intended to compensate for Germany's declining military fortunes by striking psychological and physical blows against the Allies.

British cities, including London, bore the brunt of these attacks, with the first V-1 bomb falling in June 1944 and the V-2 arriving shortly thereafter. The human toll was devastating, and the destruction caused by the rockets underscored the urgent need to neutralize their threat.

V-2 Rocket

Objective

The primary objective of Operation Crossbow was to locate, target, and destroy German facilities involved in the production, testing, and launch of the V-1 flying bombs and V-2 rockets. By crippling these sites, the Allies sought to minimize the damage inflicted on civilian populations and disrupt the Nazis' plans to use these weapons to alter the course of the war.

The operation also aimed to gather crucial intelligence on Germany's rocket technology, ensuring the Allies could devise countermeasures and prevent the widespread deployment of these advanced weapons.

Details

Phase 1: Gathering Intelligence

Operation Crossbow began with intensive intelligence-gathering efforts. British intelligence, supported by the Resistance in occupied Europe, including Poland, played a pivotal role in identifying key sites involved in the V-weapon program. Spy reports, reconnaissance flights, and captured German documents provided crucial details about the rocket facilities.

One major breakthrough came in 1943 when reconnaissance planes spotted unusual construction sites in northern France, notably Peenemünde on the Baltic Sea, where the rockets were being developed and tested. This led to the first bombing raid on Peenemünde in August 1943, marking the start of Operation Crossbow.

Phase 2: Targeting Key Facilities

The operation targeted three main types of sites:

- **Production Facilities:** Factories where the rockets were manufactured, often underground or heavily fortified to withstand aerial bombardment.
- **Launch Sites:** Fixed and mobile installations in northern France, Belgium, and the Netherlands used to fire the rockets at British cities.
- **Research and Development Centers:** Locations like Peenemünde, where scientists worked on perfecting the weapons.

Original V-2 rocket, one of 21 known to survive and found at a munitions factory near Nienburg, in April 1945.

Phase 3: Bombing Campaigns

Thousands of bombing raids were carried out by the Royal Air Force (RAF) and the United States Army Air Forces (USAAF). The Peenemünde raid was a critical early success, delaying the V-2 program by several months. However, the campaign faced significant challenges, including heavy anti-aircraft defenses and the Nazis' ability to quickly repair and relocate launch sites.

One innovative approach involved the use of the "Tallboy" and "Grand Slam" bombs, massive ordnance designed to penetrate hardened structures. These bombs were instrumental in targeting underground bunkers and production facilities.

Avro Lancaster of No. 103 Squadron RAF, launches bombing raid on the V2 assembly and launching bunker at Wizernes, France.

Phase 4: Countering the Rockets in Flight

The Allies developed defensive measures to intercept the rockets. Anti-aircraft guns and fighter planes were deployed to shoot down V-1s mid-flight, while radar technology and spotter networks helped track incoming rockets. Although these efforts had limited success against the faster V-2s, they provided some degree of protection against the V-1 threat.

Significance of Operation Crossbow

Operation Crossbow played a crucial role in mitigating the impact of Germany's V-weapon program. While it did not completely eliminate the threat, it achieved several key objectives:

- **Delaying the Rocket Program:** The bombing raids on Peenemünde and other sites significantly disrupted the production and deployment of V-weapons. Experts estimate that the Peenemünde raid alone delayed the V-2 program by six months, buying the Allies critical time to prepare for the Normandy invasion.

- **Minimizing Civilian Casualties:** Although thousands of V-1 and V-2 rockets were launched, the destruction of key facilities limited their numbers and reduced the overall death toll. Combined with defensive measures, Operation Crossbow helped save countless lives.

- **Undermining German Morale:** The campaign demonstrated the Allies' ability to strike at the heart of Nazi Germany's secret weapons program, eroding confidence in the regime's promises of technological salvation.

- **Laying the Groundwork for the Space Age:** Ironically, the intelligence gathered during Operation Crossbow contributed to post-war advancements in rocketry. Many of the scientists involved in the V-weapon program, including Wernher von Braun, later played key roles in the U.S. space program.

❖ *DID YOU KNOW*

- During the raid on Peenemünde, the Allies used specially trained Mosquito

- aircraft to drop decoy flares, confusing German anti-aircraft defenses. This tactic allowed the bombers to approach their targets with minimal losses.

- Polish intelligence officer Jan Karski smuggled information about German rocket testing to the British. His reports provided invaluable insights that guided Operation Crossbow's early phases.

- The Allies prioritized Operation Crossbow despite its immense risks. Bombers often flew missions with minimal fighter escorts, facing deadly flak and enemy fighters, because delaying the rocket program was deemed worth the high cost.

- Unlike the V-1, which could be intercepted mid-flight, the V-2 traveled faster than the speed of sound, making it impossible to detect or shoot down. This terror weapon was one of the first true ballistic missiles in history.

- The V-weapon program relied heavily on forced labor. Thousands of prisoners, many from concentration camps like Mittelbau-Dora, were subjected to inhumane conditions while working on rocket production. Their suffering remains a haunting aspect of this technological achievement.

- After the war, both the U.S. and the Soviet Union scrambled to capture German rocket scientists. Operation Crossbow indirectly contributed to this technological rivalry, as intelligence gathered on the V-weapons underscored their potential for civilian space exploration.

Significance of Operation Crossbow

Operation Crossbow was both a tactical and strategic success, though not without its limitations. The campaign disrupted the V-weapon program and reduced its impact, but it came at a high cost. Hundreds of Allied airmen lost their lives in the bombing raids, and the campaign could not prevent all rocket attacks.

Legacy of Operation Crossbow

Today the remnants of V-weapon sites, such as the preserved bunker at La Coupole in northern France, stand as stark reminders of this critical chapter in World War II history. They offer a sobering perspective on the destructive potential of technology and the enduring need for vigilance and innovation in the face of emerging threats.

10. OPERATION CHASTISE (1943) – THE DAMBUSTERS RAID

Let's look at one of the most famous and legendary operations of WWII, known as the Dambusters Raid – it was also one of the most dangerous!

Operation Chastise, famously known as the "Dambusters Raid," was a high-risk mission carried out by the Royal Air Force (RAF) on the night of May 16- 17, 1943. The primary goal was to destroy three strategically important dams in the Ruhr Valley of Germany- the Möhne, Eder, and Sorpe dams- using specially designed "bouncing bombs." These dams were crucial to the Nazi war effort, as they supplied water and power to the Ruhr Valley, Germany's industrial heartland. The mission aimed to disrupt German industrial production, damage its war economy, and lower morale by demonstrating the RAF's ability to strike at critical infrastructure.

What Was Happening in The War at This Point

World War II had entered a pivotal phase. Germany's industrial centers were working relentlessly to sustain the Nazi war machine, producing weapons, vehicles, and other materials essential for the war effort. The Ruhr Valley was the lifeline of this production, home to countless factories, steelworks, and power plants. The Allies recognized that crippling this industrial hub would slow German production, weaken their ability to sustain prolonged warfare, and provide a much-needed morale boost to Allied forces.

Objective

The idea for Operation Chastise emerged from an innovative solution to a challenging problem: how to destroy the heavily fortified dams in the Ruhr Valley. These dams were protected by anti-aircraft defenses, netting, and torpedo barriers, making traditional bombing runs ineffective. Enter Barnes Wallis, an ingenious British engineer who designed the "bouncing bomb" to overcome these obstacles. This bomb would skip across the surface of the water like a stone before hitting the dam walls and detonating underwater, where it would cause maximum damage.

Operation Chastise represented a unique convergence of technological innovation, daring strategy, and unparalleled bravery. It was entrusted to 617 Squadron, an elite group of pilots and crew formed specifically for the raid and led by 24 year old Wing Commander Guy Gibson. The squadron included British, Canadian, American, Australian and New Zealand airmen.

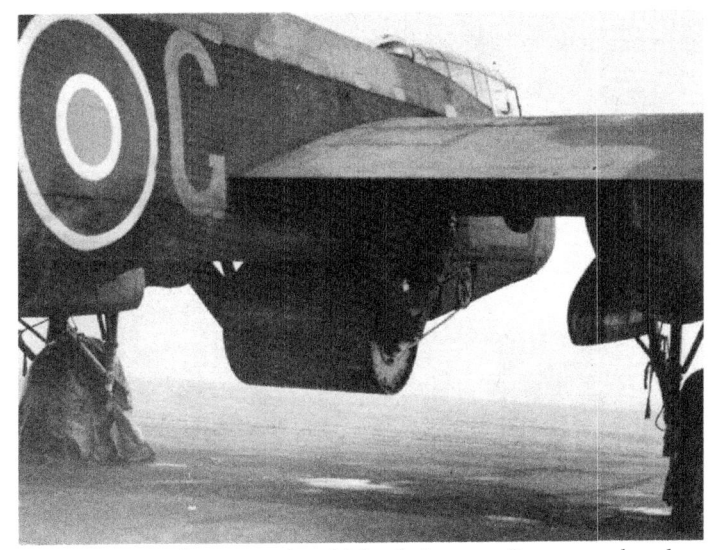

Upkeep mine (bouncing bomb) loaded onto a Lancaster bomber

Details

Preparations and Training

The success of Operation Chastise relied on precision, skill, and coordination. The 617 Squadron, nicknamed the "Dambusters," underwent intense training to prepare for the mission. They practiced low-altitude flying to evade enemy radar and rehearsed releasing the bouncing bombs from precise heights and speeds. The bombs, codenamed "Upkeep," were large cylindrical devices designed to spin backward before being dropped, ensuring they skipped across the water surface and hit their targets.

The mission's timing was also critical. The dams needed to be attacked when water levels were high enough to ensure maximum damage from the resulting floods. Additionally, the operation required moonlight to guide the pilots during their low-altitude approach.

The Raid

The mission commenced on the night of May 16, 1943, when 19 Lancaster bombers took off from RAF Scampton in Lincolnshire, England. Divided into three waves, the aircraft embarked on a perilous journey to Germany, navigating enemy defenses, searchlights, and anti-aircraft fire.

Wing Commander Guy Gibson (in door of aircraft) and his crew board their Avro Lancaster bomber

The first target was the Möhne Dam, which Wing Commander Gibson's team reached after a harrowing flight. Under heavy fire, the bombers made repeated passes, and after several attempts, one of the bouncing bombs breached the dam. The resulting floodwaters devastated the surrounding area, sweeping away factories, houses, and bridges.

The Moehne Dam before the war

The Eder Dam was the second target. Located in a deep valley, it presented unique challenges due to its difficult approach. After multiple runs, the dam was successfully breached, causing another massive flood. The Sorpe Dam, however, proved more resilient. Its earthen structure absorbed the impact of the bombs, and it remained largely intact despite valiant efforts by the squadron.

The raid came at a great cost to the Allied aircrew - of the 19 bombers that participated in the raid, 8 were shot down, resulting in the loss of 53 aircrew. Despite these losses, the mission was deemed a partial success, as it achieved its objective of disrupting German industry and morale.

The Outcome

Industrial and Economic Disruption

The destruction of the Möhne and Eder dams caused significant flooding, which disrupted industrial production and power supply in the Ruhr Valley. The floods also damaged railway lines and coal mines, temporarily paralyzing Germany's war industry.

Additionally, the destruction of the dams diverted German resources, as thousands of workers were reassigned to repair the damage and bolster the defenses of other critical infrastructure.

No. 617 Squadron practice dropping the 'Upkeep' weapon at Reculver bombing range, Kent.

However, the impact of the raid was not as long-lasting as the Allies had hoped. Germany quickly mobilized repair efforts, and production levels in the Ruhr Valley were restored within a few months. Nevertheless, the operation forced the Germans to divert attention and resources away from other fronts, indirectly aiding the broader Allied war effort.

Significance of Operation Chastise

Operation Chastise had an enormous psychological impact. For the Allies, the mission was a morale booster, showcasing the ingenuity of British engineering and the courage of RAF personnel. It also demonstrated that even Germany's most heavily defended infrastructure was vulnerable to Allied attacks.

For the Germans, the raid was a stark reminder of the Allies' growing ability to strike deep within their territory. While the damage was ultimately reparable, the psychological blow to German morale was significant, as it exposed vulnerabilities in their industrial defenses.

❖ *DID YOU KNOW*

- The bouncing bomb, designed by Sir Barnes Wallis, was an extraordinary innovation and engineering marvel. Its unique design and spinning mechanism allowed it to skip over water and evade defenses before sinking to the base of a dam wall and detonating. Wallis initially faced skepticism about his invention, but his persistence convinced military leaders of its potential.

- Barnes Wallace also designed the bombs that destroyed the Tirpitz, the V-rocket sites and much of Germany's railway network!

- Barnes Wallace was quite a remarkable man - in 1971 he designed an aircraft that could fly five times the speed of sound and needed a runway only 300 yards (275 metres) long;

- The Dambusters flew at altitudes as low as 60 feet to evade radar detection and ensure the precise delivery of the bouncing bombs. This daring tactic made the raid one of the most challenging and dangerous missions of the war.

- The distance to the dam was judged using a wooden triangular sight. The height was determined by two intersecting spotlights under the aircraft.

- Wing Commander Guy Gibson, who led the raid, demonstrated exceptional bravery and heroic leadership. Despite heavy enemy fire, Gibson made multiple bombing runs and guided his squadron through the mission. He was awarded the Victoria Cross, the highest military honor in the British armed forces, for his actions.

Wing Commander Guy P Gibson VC DSO & Bar DFC & Bar, Commanding Officer of No 617 Squadron, Royal Air Force

- The mission came at a high price. Of the 133 aircrew who participated, 53 lost their lives, and several others were captured as prisoners of war. Their sacrifices highlighted the immense courage required for such a perilous operation.

- The floods caused by the breached dams were catastrophic. Villages and towns were submerged for 50 miles and over 1,600 civilians drowned, including many forced laborers and prisoners of war. The scale of destruction underscored the devastating power of the operation.

- The bravery and skill of No. 617 Squadron earned them a place in history. They became one of the RAF's most famous units, later involved in other high-profile missions.

- The Dambusters Raid has become a symbol of wartime innovation and heroism. It inspired the 1955 film The Dam Busters, which remains one of the most celebrated depictions of World War II. The mission's theme music, composed by Eric Coates, is still widely recognized today.

The Legacy of Operation Chastise

Operation Chastise remains one of the most iconic missions of World War II, representing a unique blend of technological ingenuity, strategic daring, and individual heroism. While its immediate impact on German industry was limited, the raid showcased the Allies' ability to innovate and execute bold operations under immense pressure.

The Dambusters Raid also demonstrated the importance of targeting infrastructure in modern warfare. By disrupting critical supply chains and diverting enemy resources, the operation contributed to the larger Allied strategy of weakening the Nazi war machine from within.

Perhaps most importantly, Operation Chastise serves as a testament to the courage and determination of the men who carried it out. Their story continues to inspire generations, reminding us of the sacrifices made in the fight against tyranny.

11. OPERATION JAYWICK (1943): ATTACK ON JAPANESE SHIPPING

Here's our first operation in the war in the Pacific, targeting the Japanese. It's also an operation where all of its participants returned home safely!

Operation Jaywick, conducted in September 1943, was a covert mission by Australian and British commandos with the goal of crippling Japanese shipping in Singapore Harbor. The objective was to infiltrate the heavily guarded harbor, attach limpet mines to enemy vessels, and escape undetected. This daring raid sought to disrupt Japanese supply lines, reduce their naval capabilities, and deal a psychological blow to their dominance in Southeast Asia.

What Was Happening in The War at This Point

By 1943, the war in the Pacific was in full swing. Following Japan's aggressive expansion across Asia, the Allies were desperate to undermine Japanese dominance and regain control over the region. Singapore, which had fallen to Japanese forces in February 1942, was a key strategic location. The harbor served as a vital hub for Japanese shipping, providing essential supplies and reinforcements for their operations across the Pacific.

Objective

The Allies recognized the importance of disrupting Japanese supply lines to weaken their war effort. However, Singapore Harbor was one of the most heavily fortified and well-guarded locations in the region. A direct assault would have been suicidal, so the Allies turned to unconventional warfare. This was where Operation Jaywick came into play - a meticulously planned, high-risk mission relying on stealth, ingenuity, and courage to cripple Japanese shipping.

Details

Planning and Preparations

Operation Jaywick was the brainchild of Major Ivan Lyon of the Allied Intelligence Bureau and Lieutenant Hubert Edward "Ted" Carse of the Royal Australian Navy. Together, they developed a bold plan to use a disguised fishing vessel to transport commandos close to Singapore Harbor. From there, the team would deploy collapsible kayaks (known as "folboats") to infiltrate the harbor and plant limpet mines on Japanese ships.

The vessel chosen for the operation was the Krait, a Japanese fishing boat captured in 1941. It was refurbished and painted to blend in with local fishing vessels, complete with a Malay crew to further disguise its Allied origins. The team underwent rigorous training in folboat handling, navigation, and explosive placement. Secrecy was paramount; even high-ranking Allied officers were unaware of the mission's details.

The Krait

The Raid

On September 2, 1943, the Krait departed from Exmouth, Western Australia, with 14 men aboard - six commandos and eight crew members. The journey to Singapore took over three weeks, during which the team had to evade Japanese patrols and navigate treacherous waters. Disguised as fishermen, they passed through enemy-controlled territories without arousing suspicion.

Upon reaching a position near Singapore Harbor, the commandos launched their folboats on the night of September 24, 1943. Splitting into pairs, they paddled silently toward the harbor under the cover of darkness. Despite the presence of searchlights, patrol boats, and anti-submarine nets, the commandos successfully infiltrated the harbor.

Over the next two nights, they attached limpet mines to seven Japanese ships. The explosives were set to detonate after the commandos had retreated to safety. The resulting explosions caused significant damage, sinking or severely damaging the targeted vessels. The commandos then made their way back to the Krait, which began the perilous return journey to Australia.

The Outcome

Operation Jaywick was a resounding success. The raid destroyed an estimated 37,000 tons of Japanese shipping, including transport and cargo vessels critical to their war effort. The operation also demonstrated the vulnerability of Japanese forces in what they considered a secure stronghold, shaking their confidence and morale.

Crew of The Krait

The Japanese, unaware of the true perpetrators, launched a brutal investigation. Believing local saboteurs were responsible, they arrested and tortured hundreds of civilians in Singapore. This tragic aftermath highlighted the human cost of the mission, even as it underscored the effectiveness of Allied covert operations.

Significance of Operation Jaywick

Operation Jaywick had both immediate and long-term implications for the Allied war effort in the Pacific.

The operation was a tactical success, achieving its primary objective of disrupting Japanese shipping. The loss of vessels and supplies hampered Japan's ability to sustain its military campaigns, particularly in the face of increasing Allied pressure in the Pacific.

The rain had a psychological impact on the Japanese. The raid sent a clear message that the Allies could strike at the heart of Japanese-controlled territory, no matter how well defended. This blow to Japanese morale was significant, as it exposed weaknesses in their security measures.

Operation Jaywick paved the way for subsequent covert missions, including the ill-fated Operation Rimau in 1944. While Rimau ended in tragedy, the success of Jaywick demonstrated the value of unconventional tactics in asymmetric warfare.

The mission demonstrated the close collaboration between Australian and British forces, highlighting the importance of joint operations in achieving shared objectives and strengthening these partnerships. This partnership became a cornerstone of Allied strategy in the Pacific.

❖ *DID YOU KNOW*

- Operation Jaywick was named after a village in Essex, England, where Major Ivan Lyon had holidayed as a child. The seemingly innocuous name helped maintain the operation's secrecy.

- The Krait was a captured Japanese fishing vessel, chosen for its ability to blend in with local traffic. Its use was a masterstroke in deception, allowing the commandos to approach Singapore Harbor without arousing suspicion.

- The commandos traveled over 3,000 miles round trip in enemy-controlled waters without being detected - a testament to their skill and the effectiveness of their disguises.

- Limpet mines, used in the operation, were small, magnetized explosives designed to attach to a ship's hull. They were named after the sea creature because of their ability to cling to surfaces. The mines were detonated by timers, allowing the commandos to escape before the explosions.

- Following the raid, there were brutal Japanese reprisals. They arrested and tortured hundreds of civilians in Singapore, suspecting local resistance fighters of the sabotage. This tragic consequence highlighted the human cost of covert operations during wartime.

- Despite the overwhelming odds, all members of the Operation Jaywick team survived and returned safely to Australia. Their successful escape added to the operation's legend.

- The Krait has been preserved and is now on display at the Australian National Maritime Museum in Sydney, serving as a reminder of the bravery and ingenuity of those who served in Operation Jaywick.

- Operation Jaywick is often cited as an inspiration and precursor to modern special operations missions. Its emphasis on stealth, precision, and psychological impact has influenced the tactics of special forces worldwide.

Legacy of Operation Jaywick

Operation Jaywick remains one of the most celebrated missions in the history of Australian and British special operations. It demonstrated the effectiveness of unconventional warfare in achieving strategic objectives, even against a well-defended enemy.

The bravery and ingenuity of the commandos involved have inspired countless stories, films, and books. The raid also serves as a reminder of the sacrifices made by civilians caught in the crossfire of war, highlighting the complex ethical dilemmas of covert operations.

12. OPERATION FORTITUDE (1944): THE MASTERSTROKE OF DECEPTION

Let's look at one of the most important deception campaigns of WWII that was a crucial component in the success of D-Day.

Operation Fortitude is widely regarded as one of the greatest and most successful acts of deception in military history. Its scale, complexity, and impact were unmatched during World War II.

Among the many covert operations carried out during this war, Operation Fortitude stands as a masterstroke of deception, crucial to the success of D-Day and the ultimate Allied victory. A component of the larger Operation Bodyguard, Fortitude was designed to convince the Germans that the Allied invasion of Western Europe would occur far from its actual location in Normandy. Through a mix of ingenious tactics, fake armies, and elaborate misinformation, this operation epitomized the power of psychological warfare.

Operation Fortitude was a deception campaign of unparalleled scale, incorporating elements across land, sea, and air. Its impact on the success of D-Day, one of the most pivotal operations of the war, was immense. Without Fortitude, the invasion of Normandy—and potentially the entire Allied effort to liberate Europe—might have faltered. The operation didn't just mislead the Germans in the lead-up to the invasion; it continued to deceive them for weeks after, buying the Allies critical time to secure their position in Normandy and push forward.

An inflatable "dummy" M4 Sherman

What Was Happening in The War at This Point

The Battle for Europe

By 1944, the Allied forces had made significant advances in the Mediterranean, including victories in North Africa and Italy. However, the Western Front, critical for a direct assault on Germany, remained closed. The Soviet Union, locked in a brutal struggle on the Eastern Front, was pressuring the Allies to open a second front to relieve the burden on Soviet forces. The planned invasion of Normandy would achieve this goal, but its success hinged on catching the Germans off guard.

The Atlantic Wall and the German Dilemma

The Germans had fortified France's coastline with an extensive network of bunkers, artillery, and obstacles known as the Atlantic Wall. Adolf Hitler and his generals were aware of an impending Allied invasion but were unsure where it would occur. The logical choice seemed to be Pas-de-Calais, the narrowest point between Britain and France, which would allow for easier resupply and reinforcement. This assumption became the foundation for Operation Fortitude's elaborate deception.

Objective

The primary goal of Operation Fortitude was to mislead the Germans about the location, timing, and scale of the D-Day invasion. By creating the illusion of an impending assault on other regions - particularly Pas-de-Calais and Norway - the Allies aimed to divert German forces from Normandy, leaving it less defended and easier to breach. This deception was vital to the success of Operation Overlord, the codename for the D-Day landings, as it enabled the Allies to establish a foothold in Nazi-occupied France.

Details

Operation Fortitude was divided into two complementary parts, each targeting a different region and achieving distinct objectives.

Fortitude North: Norway Deception

Fortitude North aimed to convince the Germans that an Allied invasion force would land in Norway. The Allies created a fictitious invasion force, complete with fake troop movements, to keep German divisions stationed in Scandinavia. This effort involved the creation of phantom armies. Inflatable tanks and dummy landing craft were positioned in Scotland to simulate preparations for an invasion of Norway.

The Allies also used fake radio traffic. Radio operators transmitted fabricated messages to suggest troop movements toward Scandinavia.

Double Agents were used, such as the Allied spy, Juan Pujol García (codenamed Garbo), who fed misinformation to German intelligence, reinforcing the illusion of a Norwegian invasion.

The result? German forces remained stationed in Norway, far from the true invasion site in Normandy.

Fortitude South: The Pas-de-Calais Deception

Fortitude South was designed to mislead the Germans into believing that the primary Allied invasion would occur at Pas-de-Calais, the shortest distance (21 miles) across the English Channel and a logical launchpad for an invasion.

Dummy landing craft used as decoys in south-eastern England harbours

This deception involved the creation of a completely fictitious army - The First United States Army Group (FUSAG)! This was a made up army group, supposedly commanded by General George S. Patton, was 'stationed' in southeastern England, in Kent. Patton's reputation as a brilliant and aggressive leader made the deception more convincing. While FUSAG wasn't real, the Allies went to extraordinary lengths to make it appear so, using a combination of props, disinformation, and strategic positioning. FUSAG was designed to look like an enormous military formation, of 11 Divisions, including several armored divisions, and 150,000 troops – a similar number to those that actually landed on the Normandy beaches.

Soldiers working on these deceptions were told to walk into nearby towns waring different uniforms, making it looks to any German spies, that there were lots of different units stationed nearby.

Around 500 inflatable tanks were positioned in fields to be spotted by German reconnaissance. These props created the illusion of a massive force poised to cross the Channel at Pas-de-Calais. Wooden structures mimicked troop encampments, supply depots, and vehicle parks. Fake planes and airfields were created, with the planes made of plywood.

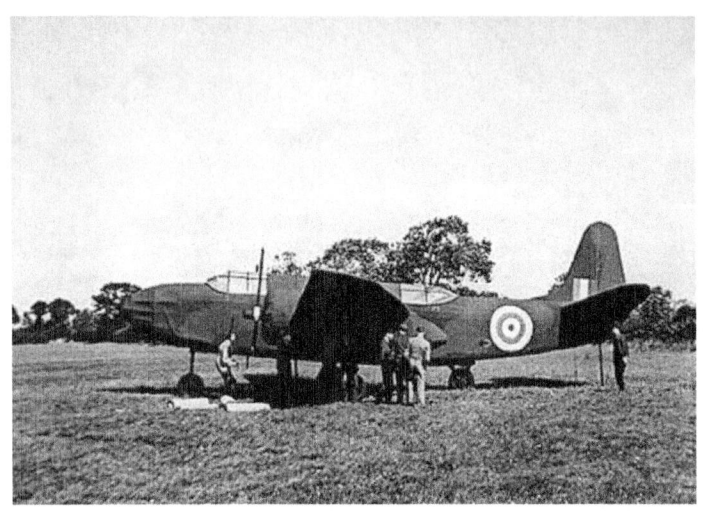

Dummy aircraft

As the Fortitude North, the Allies generated fake radio communications to simulate the logistics and operations of a large army group. These messages were intentionally intercepted by German intelligence.

Again, double agents and false reports were used. Agents were crucial to the success of so many operations. Fortitude was successful in large part to the actions of Juan Pujol, a double-agent known as 'Garbo'. Between January 1944 and D-Day, Garbo sent over 500 radio messages to the Germans—sometimes more than twenty in a single day! To maintain his cover as a trusted German informant, Garbo and his handlers decided to give the Germans some limited information about the Normandy invasion. But here's the twist: they sent the message too late for the Germans to do anything about it.

Then, three days after D-Day, Garbo delivered another critical message. He told the Germans that the Normandy landings were just a distraction and that the 'real' invasion was still coming at Calais. This report went straight to Hitler, who believed it completely. He ordered German forces in Calais to stay put, even as the Allies were advancing in Normandy.

Juan Pujol García

Incredibly, two months after D-Day, there were still more German troops stationed in Calais than there had been on the beaches of Normandy on D-Day itself. This delay was a game-changer, giving the Allies the breathing room they needed to establish a strong foothold in Normandy and continue their march across Europe.

A Landing Craft disembarks troops of the U.S. Army's First Division on the morning of June 6, 1944 (D-Day) at Omaha Beach.

The Outcome

On June 6, 1944, the Allies launched the largest amphibious assault in history on the beaches of Normandy – many miles from Calais!

Thanks to Operation Fortitude, the Germans were unprepared for the attack. Believing that the Normandy invasion was merely a diversion, German High Command delayed sending reinforcements to the region, expecting the 'real' invasion at Pas-de-Calais. Even weeks after D-Day, German forces remained concentrated in Calais, unable to respond effectively to the Allied advance.

❖ *DID YOU KNOW*

- Juan Pujol García was a Double Agent 'Extraordinaire'! Known by the codename Garbo, García was a Spanish double agent who played a pivotal role in Fortitude. He fed a steady stream of fabricated intelligence to the Germans, earning their trust to such an extent that they awarded him the Iron Cross for his 'service' - unaware he was working for the Allies all along. Pujol had the distinction of receiving honors from both sides of the war - the British awarded him the MBE!

- The inflatable tanks and trucks used in Fortitude were so realistic that German reconnaissance planes reported them as genuine. These props were moved periodically to mimic troop movements, adding to the illusion of a large force.
- Fortitude's deception was so effective that some Germans believed the fictitious FUSAG had suffered massive casualties during the Normandy campaign, explaining why it did not follow up with an invasion at Calais.
- Operation Fortitude involved some bold risks, one of the most daring being the use of General Hans Cramer, a captured German officer. Cramer, who had led the Afrika Korps, was captured in May 1943 and, due to his poor health, was exchanged back to Germany in 1944. During his captivity, the Allies saw an opportunity to deceive the Germans.

In May 1944, Cramer was invited to dinner with General Patton, who was introduced as the commander of the First U.S. Army Group (FUSAG). Patton repeatedly mentioned the Pas de Calais to reinforce the illusion. Afterward, Cramer was driven through what he believed were towns in southeast England, passing large numbers of troops and military equipment. He was convinced that the massive buildup was for the invasion of Pas de Calais.

In reality, he had been driven through southwest England, where the real preparations for Normandy were taking place, passing huge numbers of troops. Road signs were hidden so he didn't actually know where he was. He was shocked by the extent of the build-up of troops that he saw.

Cramer was sent to neutral Sweden, where he reported immediately reported to the Germans, telling them about his dinner with Patton and the 'huge buildup' he had witnessed in 'Kent'. His report helped convince the German high command that the Allies would land at Pas de Calais, reinforcing the success of the deception and diverting German forces away from Normandy.

Significance of Operation Fortitude

Operation Fortitude was not merely a tactical success; it was a strategic masterpiece that demonstrated the Allies' ingenuity and adaptability. Its impact extended far beyond the beaches of Normandy, playing a pivotal role in the success of the D-Day landings on June 6, 1944, which marked a turning point in the war. By securing a foothold in Western Europe, the Allies were able to begin the liberation of Nazi-occupied territories. By doing some, Operation Fortitude cemented its place in history as one of the greatest deceptions ever conceived.

In the end, the success of Operation Fortitude underscores a fundamental truth of warfare: victory often depends not only on strength and firepower but also on the ability to outthink and outmaneuver one's opponent. By exploiting German assumptions and using deception as a weapon, the Allies turned the tide of World War II and paved the way for the liberation of Europe.

The Legacy of Operation Fortitude

Turning the Tide of the War

Operation Fortitude's success was instrumental in ensuring the success of the Normandy invasion. By diverting German forces and spreading confusion, it allowed the Allies to secure a foothold in France, leading to the liberation of Paris and the eventual collapse of Nazi Germany.

A Testament to Psychological Warfare

Fortitude demonstrated the power of deception in warfare. It proved that battles could be won not just on the battlefield, but in the minds of the enemy. The operation's success highlighted the importance of intelligence, creativity, and strategic planning in modern warfare.

Inspiration for Modern Military Strategy

The principles of deception and misinformation employed in Operation Fortitude continue to influence military strategy today. From fake maneuvers to cyber deception, the lessons of Fortitude remain relevant in an era of advanced technology and information warfare.

13. OPERATION JEDBURGH (1944): A CRUCIAL LINK IN THE D-DAY STRATEGY

Now for a daring and dangerous operation behind enemy lines in occupied France!

As the Allied forces prepared for the massive D-Day invasion of Nazi-occupied France in June 1944, the success of the operation hinged on more than just the storming of beaches. Disrupting German supply lines, communication networks, and reinforcements inland was critical to ensuring the invasion's success. Enter Operation Jedburgh, a daring and unconventional mission where Allied teams were parachuted into France to aid and organize the French Resistance. These teams, known as "Jeds," played a pivotal role in the success of the Allied invasion by sowing chaos behind enemy lines, in France, Belgium and the Netherlands.

Objective

The primary goal of Operation Jedburgh was to organize, arm, and assist local French Resistance groups in disrupting German operations before and during D-Day. This included sabotage, ambushes, and cutting communication lines to delay German reinforcements from reaching the frontlines.

By 1944, the Allies recognized the value of guerrilla warfare as a complement to conventional military operations. The French Resistance, though committed to the cause, lacked coordination and resources. The Special Operations Executive (SOE) and the Office of Strategic Services (OSS) developed Operation Jedburgh to bridge this gap, sending highly trained teams to act as liaisons between the Resistance and the Allied command.

Operation Jedburgh was one of the earliest examples of modern unconventional warfare. Its success required close collaboration between British, American, and Free French forces.

Jedburghs get instructions from Briefing Officer in London flat

Details

Formation of Jedburgh Teams

- Each Jedburgh team consisted of three members - a commander (usually British, American, or Free French), a radio operator to maintain contact with Allied headquarters, and a native French speaker to liaise with the Resistance.

- Teams were equipped with weapons, radios, explosives, and basic supplies. Their small size allowed them to operate covertly.

- The Jeds received extensive foreign language instruction, as well as training in parachuting, amphibious operations, skiing, mountain climbing, radio operations, Morse code, small arms, navigation, hand-to-hand combat, explosives, and espionage tactics.

Deployment

The first Jedburgh teams parachuted into France in the days leading up to D-Day (June 6, 1944). They landed in remote areas, often under the cover of darkness, to avoid detection by German patrols. On total, over 90 teams parachuted into France.

Jedburghs in front of B-24 just before night at Area T, Harrington Airdrome, England

Upon landing, the teams sought out local Resistance groups, who were often operating in secrecy and under constant threat of betrayal. The Jeds worked to gain their trust, share intelligence, and provide leadership.

The Jeds coordinated the delivery of Allied supplies, including weapons, explosives, and radios, to Resistance fighters. These supplies were critical for conducting sabotage operations.

Disrupting German Operations

Resistance groups, guided by the Jeds, destroyed railway lines, derailed trains, and ambushed German convoys.

They targeted key infrastructure such as bridges, communication hubs, and supply depots, significantly delaying German reinforcements to the Normandy beaches.

Challenges and Risks

Hostile Environment

France in 1944 was heavily controlled by the Nazis. German patrols, collaborators, and informants posed constant threats. The Jeds often operated in isolated areas, relying on their wits and the loyalty of local Resistance members.

Betrayal and Capture

The risk of betrayal was high. Some Jedburgh members were captured, tortured, and executed by the Nazis. Yet, their bravery under duress often inspired local Resistance fighters to continue the fight.

Communication Issues

Maintaining contact with Allied headquarters was critical but challenging. The radio operators, often working in makeshift shelters, faced difficulties with signal interference and the constant threat of being triangulated by German forces.

Outcome

Operation Jedburgh proved to be a resounding success, achieving its primary objectives and contributing significantly to the success of D-Day. Jedburgh teams carried out similar operations with other Allied Special Forces in Norway, Italy, Burma, Malaya, Borneo, Indonesia, China, and Indo-China

Delaying German Reinforcements

The sabotage efforts organized by the Jeds and the Resistance created chaos for the German military. Train derailments, roadblocks, and destroyed bridges forced German units to divert resources to repair infrastructure, slowing their response to the Allied invasion. By the time German reinforcements arrived at the Normandy beaches, the Allies had already established a strong foothold.

'The disruption of enemy rail communications, the harassing of German road moves and the continual and increasing strain placed on German security services throughout occupied Europe... played a very considerable part in our complete and final victory.'

General Dwight Eisenhower, Supreme Allied Commander - May 1945

Boosting Morale

The presence of Allied operatives in occupied France gave the Resistance a much-needed morale boost. It signaled that the liberation of France was imminent and that their efforts were part of a larger Allied strategy.

Paving the Way for Liberation

The Jeds helped turn the scattered Resistance groups into a coordinated force, ensuring they played a vital role in the liberation of France.

❖ *DID YOU KNOW*

- Captured Jeds were known to feign ignorance and destroy their radios or codes to protect Allied secrets. Their courage under interrogation became legendary.

- The motto of the Jedburgh teams was: "Surprise, kill, and vanish."

- "Wanted: Volunteers for immediate overseas assignment. Knowledge of French or another European language preferred; Willingness and ability to qualify as a parachutist necessary; Likelihood of a dangerous mission guaranteed." This message was broadcast at military bases across the U.S. to recruit commandos for Operation Jeburgh.

- In one instance, a Jedburgh team helped a Resistance group destroy a German train carrying tanks and ammunition, derailing it in spectacular fashion.

- Teams would siphon axle oil from German rail transport cars and replace it with abrasive grease to disable them. This prevented the 2nd SS Panzer Division from reaching Normandy before the Allied breakout.

- The Jedburgh teams carried silk maps, compasses hidden in buttons, and escape kits with cyanide pills in case of capture.

- These were life-and-death operations. Major John Bonsal, one of the first Jedburghs dropped into Brittany, was stopped at a German checkpoint, identified, and executed.

- In one remarkable incident, a Jedburgh team parachuted into a remote French village just days before D-Day. Working with the local Resistance, they fortified the village and conducted guerrilla attacks on German convoys in the area. Despite being outnumbered, the Jeds and the Resistance fighters held off a German retaliation until Allied reinforcements arrived.

- Several Jeds made daring escapes after their missions were compromised. One operator, after being separated from his team, trekked over 50 miles through enemy territory, evading German patrols, before reuniting with the Resistance.

- Even when facing certain death, Jedburgh members refused to abandon their mission. Captured operatives often misled the Nazis with false information, protecting both the Resistance and Allied plans.

Legacy of Operation Jedburgh

Many Jedburgh veterans went on to serve in newly formed special operations units, including the U.S. Army Green Berets and the British SAS.

Operation Jedburgh laid the groundwork for modern special operations. The integration of local resistance fighters, the emphasis on guerrilla tactics, and the use of small, highly trained teams became a model for future unconventional warfare strategies.

By empowering the French Resistance and sowing chaos behind enemy lines, the Jedburgh teams played a vital role in the success of D-Day and the eventual liberation of France.

14. OPERATION SUNRISE (1945): SECRET NEGOTIATIONS THAT HASTENED THE END OF WORLD WAR II

This is an operation unlike those we've already covered – this was an attempt to shorten the war through negotiation and not by force.

Operation Sunrise was a pivotal, though less well-known, event that demonstrated the power of secret negotiations and intelligence work in shaping the outcome of World War II.

Operation Sunrise was a clandestine effort to secure the early surrender of German forces in Northern Italy during the final months of World War II. Its primary goal was to shorten the conflict in Europe, reduce casualties, and disrupt Nazi plans for prolonged resistance. By negotiating with high-ranking German officials, the Allies sought to undermine Hitler's authority and prevent unnecessary destruction in the region.

What Was Happening in The War at This Point

By early 1945, the war in Europe was reaching its conclusion. The Allied forces were advancing on multiple fronts, with Soviet troops pushing into Eastern Europe and Western Allied forces moving through Germany. Despite their inevitable defeat, some German commanders sought to prolong the war, potentially allowing remnants of the Nazi regime to regroup or negotiate a more favorable outcome.

Northern Italy, controlled by German forces under Field Marshal Albert Kesselring, was a key region of resistance. The terrain, including the formidable Alps, provided a natural defensive advantage, and German troops were prepared to fight fiercely. An extended conflict in Italy could cost thousands of lives and delay the war's end.

Field Marshal Albert Kesselring, commander of the German ground forces in Italy, 1943–1945

Objective

Operation Sunrise emerged from these circumstances as a bold initiative to shorten the war. Orchestrated by the U.S. Office of Strategic Services (OSS) - the precursor to the CIA - and Swiss intermediaries, it involved secret negotiations with German officials, including SS General Karl Wolff. The operation's success depended on convincing Wolff and his subordinates to bypass Hitler's orders and surrender unconditionally.

Details

The first steps of Operation Sunrise were taken in February 1945, when Swiss intelligence officer Max Waibel, acting as an intermediary, facilitated contact between the OSS and German representatives. The negotiations were led by Allen Dulles, the head of the OSS in Switzerland, who operated with discretion to avoid detection by both

German and Allied authorities.

General Karl Wolff, who served as the SS Commander in Italy, became a pivotal figure in the talks. Wolff, aware of Germany's impending defeat, sought to save his forces from destruction and secure his position in a post-war world. This pragmatic self-interest created an opening for negotiations.

Karl Wolff, SS-Gruppenführer

Switzerland's neutrality and geographic proximity made it an ideal location for secret diplomacy. Meetings were held in Zurich and Bern, with Swiss officials providing logistical support and safeguarding the confidentiality of the discussions.

The negotiations were fraught with challenges and risks. Allied leaders, particularly Soviet Premier Joseph Stalin, viewed such talks with suspicion, fearing they would undermine the broader goal of unconditional surrender. The possibility of a separate peace with Germany in Italy risked creating tensions among the Allies.

To manage these risks, Dulles ensured that the talks remained focused on a localized surrender in Italy, explicitly avoiding broader political agreements.

Allen Dulles

After weeks of covert meetings, Wolff agreed to the terms of surrender. However, implementing the agreement was complicated by Hitler's control over German commanders. Wolff and other officers had to act against direct orders from Berlin, risking their lives and careers.

The Outcome

On May 2, 1945, following intense negotiations and strategic maneuvering, German forces, numbering 900,000, in Northern Italy surrendered to the Allies. This marked one of the earliest localized German surrenders and significantly reduced hostilities in the region. Just days later, on May 7, Germany's unconditional surrender ended the war in Europe.

Significance of Operation Sunrise

Operation Sunrise had profound implications for the war effort and post-war geopolitics.

By securing the early surrender of German forces in Northern Italy, Operation Sunrise hastened the end of the war in Europe. This saved countless lives and minimized destruction in a region already devastated by years of conflict.

It demonstrated Allied unity. Despite initial Soviet mistrust, the operation ultimately aligned with the broader Allied goal of unconditional German surrender. It underscored the Allies' ability to coordinate complex, high-stakes negotiations even in the war's chaotic final months.

It led to an erosion of Nazi authority. The success of Operation Sunrise highlighted cracks within the Nazi hierarchy. By negotiating directly with Allied representatives, German commanders like Wolff demonstrated their willingness to defy Hitler, further weakening his control.

❖ DID YOU KNOW

- Allen Dulles, who later became the first civilian director of the CIA, demonstrated exceptional diplomatic and strategic skills during Operation Sunrise. His ability to navigate the complex web of German politics and Allied diplomacy was instrumental to the mission's success.

- General Karl Wolff's participation in the operation was a daring act of defiance and a high stakes gamble. If discovered, he risked execution for treason by the Nazi regime. Wolff's decision to negotiate reflects the desperation and pragmatism of German leaders in the war's final days.

- The operation nearly caused a rift among the Allies. Stalin feared that separate negotiations in Italy might lead to a Western Allied-German alliance against the Soviet Union. The issue was so contentious that it was discussed at the Yalta Conference, where Roosevelt and Churchill reassured Stalin of their commitment to unconditional surrender.

- Switzerland's role in facilitating the negotiations demonstrated the unique advantages of its neutral status. The country's ability to mediate between warring parties highlights the importance of diplomacy in wartime.

- The surrender in Northern Italy not only saved lives but also protected cultural landmarks and treasures in the region, including Florence and Venice, from potential destruction during prolonged fighting.

- The operation's name, Sunrise, symbolized hope and new beginnings, reflecting its aim to bring the war closer to an end.

Legacy of Operation Sunrise

Operation Sunrise stands as a remarkable example of wartime diplomacy and strategic negotiation. Through careful planning, bold decision-making, and collaboration between intelligence operatives and German commanders, the operation achieved its objective of an early surrender in Northern Italy. Its success contributed to the swift conclusion of World War II in Europe, sparing countless lives and paving the way for the rebuilding of a devastated continent.

In hindsight, Operation Sunrise illustrates the complexities of war, where battles are fought not only on the front lines but also in the shadows of diplomacy and intelligence. It remains a testament to the ingenuity and resolve of those who worked tirelessly to bring peace to a world engulfed in conflict.

15. OPERATION PASTORIUS (1942): A FAILED GERMAN SABOTAGE MISSION ON U.S. SOIL

It was not only the Allies who had secret operations, the Germans had their own too!

Operation Pastorius was planned with the primary goal of disrupting the U.S. war effort by sabotaging key industries, infrastructure, and economic targets. The mission aimed to weaken American morale and hamper its ability to produce the resources and equipment needed for World War II. By targeting vital war-related facilities and transportation networks, Germany hoped to delay U.S. mobilization and shift the balance of power in their favor.

What Was Happening in The War at This Point

By mid-1942, the United States had entered World War II following the attack on Pearl Harbor. As the U.S. rapidly mobilized its industrial base to support the Allied war effort, German military leaders recognized the critical role American industry played in supplying weapons, vehicles, and equipment. Factories, railroads, bridges, and ports became key targets for disruption.

Objective

Nazi Germany, under Adolf Hitler's orders, devised Operation Pastorius as part of a broader strategy to bring the war to American soil. It was one of the few direct attempts by Germany to strike within the continental United States. Hitler and his commanders believed that a well-coordinated sabotage campaign could disrupt the production of military supplies, create panic among the civilian population, and force the U.S. to divert resources to homeland security.

Details

Recruitment and Training

The German military selected eight operatives for the mission. These men were mostly expatriates of German descent who had spent time in the United States and were familiar with American culture, language, and geography. They were recruited with promises of substantial rewards for their service to the Reich.

In the spring of 1942, the operatives underwent rigorous training in sabotage techniques, including bomb-making, demolition, and covert operations. Training took place at a secret facility in Germany, where they practiced placing explosives, setting fires, and targeting industrial equipment. Each man was also given a false identity, forged documents, and a cover story to blend into American society upon arrival.

The Mission

The plan called for the saboteurs to land on American shores via German submarines (U-boats) and split into teams to carry out coordinated attacks on high-value targets. Their objectives included:

- Aluminum and magnesium factories, critical for aircraft production.
- Railroads and bridges, essential for transporting goods and troops.
- Power plants, water systems, and other infrastructure vital to the war effort.

Each team was equipped with explosives, incendiary devices, and detailed instructions for their sabotage targets. They carried large sums of cash to fund their operations and purchase additional materials as needed.

Landing on U.S. Soil

On the night of June 13, 1942, the first group of operatives landed on a beach near Amagansett, New York, transported by the German submarine U-202. Dressed as civilian fishermen, they buried their explosives and other equipment in the sand and planned to head inland to begin their mission. However, their arrival did not go unnoticed.

Seaman John Cullen, a member of the U.S. Coast Guard, was patrolling the beach when he encountered the group. Sensing something suspicious, Cullen questioned their purpose. One of the operatives, George Dasch, attempted to bribe Cullen with

$260 to keep quiet. Cullen feigned compliance but immediately reported the encounter, prompting a swift response from U.S. authorities.

All eight operatives after their capture

A second group of saboteurs landed four days later, near Ponte Vedra Beach, Florida, transported by the submarine U-584. This team aimed to target sites in the southeastern United States. However, their arrival was similarly ill-fated.

The Outcome

Despite the initial secrecy, Operation Pastorius began to fall apart almost immediately. George Dasch, the leader of the New York team, had a change of heart after the landing. He decided to defect to the U.S. authorities, perhaps motivated by fear, guilt, or personal ambition. Dasch traveled to Washington, D.C., and turned himself in to the FBI, revealing the details of the operation.

With Dasch's cooperation, the FBI quickly apprehended the remaining operatives in New York and Florida. The men were arrested before they could carry out any acts of sabotage. The explosives, equipment, and plans they had brought with them were seized, neutralizing the threat entirely.

Aftermath and Impact of Operation Pastorius

- **Failure of the Mission:** Operation Pastorius was an unequivocal failure. None of the intended sabotage targets were attacked, and the mission ended with the arrest of all eight operatives. The Germans' hopes of striking a blow against American industry and morale were dashed.

- **Trial and Execution:** The captured saboteurs were tried by a military tribunal under President Franklin D. Roosevelt's orders. Six of the men were sentenced to death and executed in the electric chair on August 8, 1942. George Dasch and one other operative, Ernst Burger, received reduced sentences for their cooperation and were deported to Germany after the war.

- **Strengthening Homeland Security:** Operation Pastorius underscored the vulnerability of the U.S. to sabotage and espionage. In response, the government bolstered coastal defenses, tightened immigration and travel restrictions, and increased surveillance of suspected Axis sympathizers.

- **Nazi Germany's Reputation:** The mission's failure damaged the reputation of German intelligence services, exposing weaknesses in their ability to execute covert operations. It also reinforced the resolve of the Allies to counter Axis espionage efforts.

Significance of Operation Pastorius

While Operation Pastorius was a failure, its significance lies in the lessons it provided for both sides during the war. For Germany, it highlighted the challenges of executing covert operations on foreign soil and the risks of relying on operatives with divided loyalties. For the United States, it underscored the need for vigilance against espionage and sabotage, leading to stronger homeland security measures.

❖ *DID YOU KNOW*

- The explosives and equipment buried on the beach in Amagansett were discovered by the Coast Guard after Dasch's confession. Among the items were incendiary devices disguised as lumps of coal, designed to blend in with other fuel and ignite industrial machinery.

- John Cullen, the Coast Guardsman who first encountered the saboteurs, played a pivotal role in thwarting the operation. His quick thinking and bravery ensured that U.S. authorities acted before the plot could progress.

- George Dasch reportedly called the FBI headquarters directly, saying, "I am a saboteur." His defection was one of the most dramatic elements of the operation, turning the mission into a cautionary tale of betrayal within German ranks.

- Adolf Hitler was reportedly enraged by the mission's failure and ordered a halt to further sabotage operations in the U.S. The debacle of Operation Pastorius marked the end of direct German attempts to infiltrate American territory during the war.

- The operatives trained at a secret facility in Germany that mimicked American conditions, complete with mock-ups of U.S. factories and infrastructure. Despite this preparation, the mission was undone by human error and divided loyalties.

- The trial of the saboteurs was one of the few military tribunals conducted on U.S. soil during World War II. Its proceedings and swift justice highlighted the severity with which the U.S. viewed acts of sabotage and espionage.

Legacy of Operation Pastorius

Operation Pastorius is a reminder of the human factors that can influence the outcome of military missions. The defection of George Dasch, whether driven by conscience or self-interest, was a critical turning point that ensured the plot's failure. His actions, coupled with the quick response of U.S. authorities, demonstrated the importance of individual decisions in shaping the course of history.

Operation Pastorius is a cautionary tale of espionage gone wrong. Its failure did little to change the trajectory of World War II, but it remains a fascinating episode in the history of covert operations. From the bravery of John Cullen to the betrayal of George Dasch, the mission encapsulates the complexity of wartime intrigue and the high stakes of sabotage efforts. Although it achieved none of its objectives, Operation Pastorius is a reminder of the resilience and determination of those who worked to protect the United States during a time of global conflict.

16. OPERATION GREIF (1944): A TALE OF DECEPTION AND CHAOS

This is another German operation, an attempt at deception to disrupt the Allied advance in Europe.

The German military, known for its resourcefulness and audacity during World War II, launched Operation Greif in December 1944 as part of the broader Battle of the Bulge offensive. This covert operation aimed to infiltrate and confuse Allied forces by deploying German commandos disguised as American soldiers. Although it achieved mixed results, Operation Greif remains one of the war's most intriguing examples of psychological warfare and deception.

What Was Happening in The War at This Point

By late 1944, the tide of World War II had decisively turned against Germany. The Allies had liberated much of France and were advancing steadily towards the German heartland. In the east, the Soviet Union was closing in on Berlin. Facing overwhelming odds, Hitler launched a desperate counteroffensive in the Ardennes region, hoping to split the Allied forces and force a negotiated peace.

The Battle of the Bulge, which began in December 1944, was Germany's last major offensive on the Western Front. It involved a surprise attack on the thinly defended Ardennes forest, aiming to recapture the port of Antwerp and cripple the Allied supply chain. Operation Greif was conceived as a key component of this offensive, designed to exploit the element of surprise and maximize the chaos caused by the sudden German assault.

American infantrymen of the 290th Regiment fight in fresh snowfall during Battle of the Bulge, near Amonines, Belgium

Objective

The main goal of Operation Greif was to sow confusion and disrupt the coordination of Allied forces during the Ardennes offensive. By infiltrating Allied lines, the Germans hoped to:

- **Create Chaos:** German commandos, disguised in American uniforms, would spread misinformation, alter road signs, and sabotage critical infrastructure.

- **Undermine Morale:** The presence of "enemy within" was intended to erode the confidence and trust of Allied troops.

- **Facilitate Strategic Advances:** By disrupting Allied communications and supply routes, Operation Greif aimed to give German forces a tactical advantage in the Battle of the Bulge.

This bold plan reflected Adolf Hitler's belief in the power of unconventional tactics to turn the tide of the war.

Details

Planning and Leadership

Operation Greif was led by Otto Skorzeny, a German SS officer famous for his audacious rescue of Italian dictator Benito Mussolini in 1943. Charismatic and resourceful, Skorzeny was tasked with organizing and commanding the operation.

Otto Skorzeny, Waffen SS and security service

The plan involved recruiting German soldiers who spoke fluent English and training them to adopt American mannerisms, accents, and military protocols. These commandos were issued American uniforms, weapons, and vehicles, some of which were captured during previous battles.

To ensure the mission's success, Skorzeny established the 150th Panzer Brigade, a specially formed unit consisting of approximately 3,000 men. Among them, a smaller group of about 150 soldiers was selected for the infiltration missions.

Execution

Operation Greif was launched in mid-December 1944, coinciding with the start of the Battle of the Bulge. Disguised German commandos infiltrated Allied lines, where they carried out a variety of disruptive activities:

- Spreading Misinformation: Commandos provided false directions to Allied troops, leading them away from key objectives or into German ambushes.

- Sabotaging Infrastructure: Roads, bridges, and communication lines were targeted to impede Allied movements and logistics.

- Creating Panic: Rumors were deliberately spread to sow distrust among Allied forces.

One particularly damaging rumor suggested that German commandos were planning to assassinate General Dwight D. Eisenhower, the Supreme Allied Commander. This led to heightened security measures and further disrupted Allied operations.

Eisenhower addressing 502nd Parachute Infantry Regiment of the 101st Airborne Division, before D-Day.

Challenges

Despite its ambitious goals, Operation Greif faced significant challenges such as the language barrier. While the commandos were well-trained, their English was not always flawless. Subtle accents, unfamiliarity with American slang, and an inability to convincingly answer detailed questions often exposed them.

Once Allied forces became aware of the operation, they implemented strict security measures, including questioning soldiers about trivia (such as baseball scores) that the Germans would likely not know.

Outcome

Although Operation Greif caused temporary confusion, it failed to achieve its broader strategic objectives and had limited impact.

Many German commandos were captured, including several who were executed as spies under the Geneva Conventions.

Significance of Operation Greif

Operation Greif created moments of chaos and uncertainty, delaying Allied responses to the German offensive. However, these disruptions were short-lived and did not significantly alter the outcome of the Battle of the Bulge.

The operation has a psychological impact on Allied troops, with increased levels of paranoia. Soldiers became wary of anyone who seemed suspicious, and trust within units was temporarily strained. The rumored assassination plot against Eisenhower further intensified the atmosphere of fear.

Despite its limited success, Operation Greif demonstrated the lengths to which Germany was willing to go to exploit unconventional tactics. The operation highlighted both the creativity and the desperation of the German war effort in its final stages.

Operation Greif underscored the importance of intelligence, counterintelligence, and psychological warfare in modern military operations. It also illustrated the risks and limitations of deception tactics, particularly when facing a vigilant and adaptable opponent.

▫▫*DID YOU KNOW*

- One of the most extraordinary aspects of Operation Greif was the rumor that German commandos planned to assassinate General Eisenhower. This led to unprecedented security measures, with Eisenhower confined to his headquarters under heavy guard for weeks. The rumor, though unfounded, demonstrated the psychological impact of the operation.

- To root out infiltrators, Allied soldiers devised impromptu tests involving American pop culture, sports, and slang. For example, suspected spies were asked to name the capital of Illinois (Springfield, not Chicago) or identify famous baseball players.

- When captured German commandos were sentenced to execution, one of them reportedly said, "I die with a clear conscience, having done my duty." This highlighted the dedication and resolve of the operatives, despite the moral ambiguity of their mission.

- Otto Skorzeny, the mastermind of Operation Greif, became a controversial figure after the war. Although acquitted of war crimes related to the operation, he remained a divisive figure, with some viewing him as a brilliant tactician and others as a ruthless opportunist.

- The operation's use of American uniforms violated the laws of war, exposing captured commandos to execution as spies. This ethical and legal dilemma remains a point of debate among historians.

Legacy of Operation Greif

Operation Greif was an audacious attempt to turn the tide of war through deception and psychological warfare. Led by the charismatic Otto Skorzeny, the operation embodied both the ingenuity and the desperation of the German military in the closing months of World War II.

While it succeeded in causing temporary confusion and paranoia among Allied forces, it ultimately failed to achieve its strategic objectives. The Battle of the Bulge ended in a decisive Allied victory, marking the beginning of the end for Nazi Germany.

Nevertheless, Operation Greif remains a fascinating chapter in military history, offering valuable lessons on the complexities of warfare and the power of psychological operations.

17. OPERATION BERNHARD: THE NAZI PLAN TO FORGE CHAOS

Here's a very unusual operation, and an example of economic warfare, and also one of the largest counterfeiting schemes in history!

Operation Bernhard was a covert Nazi scheme to forge British banknotes during World War II. Spearheaded by the German SS, the operation aimed to destabilize the British economy by flooding it with counterfeit currency, undermining its financial stability, and weakening the Allied war effort. The ambitious plan also had a secondary aim of using the forged currency to fund German intelligence operations.

What Was Happening in The War at This Point

By the time Operation Bernhard was conceived in 1942, the war had escalated into a global conflict with devastating economic consequences for all involved. Nazi Germany was seeking innovative methods to cripple its enemies beyond conventional military tactics. The British economy, central to funding Allied efforts, was an attractive target.

Objective

At the heart of Britain's wartime financial strength was the pound sterling, one of the most respected currencies globally. The Nazis theorized that destabilizing the pound would not only create economic turmoil in Britain but also erode trust in its financial systems internationally. This attack on the financial infrastructure would act as a psychological blow to British morale while reducing its ability to fund the war effort.

Operation Bernhard was part of a broader Nazi strategy to exploit economic warfare as a tool to weaken Allied resistance. Alongside physical battles, the Nazis sought to undermine Britain through espionage, propaganda, and sabotage. This operation, however, would become infamous for its audacity, scale, and its legacy as one of the most significant counterfeiting operations in history.

Details

Origins and Planning

The idea for Operation Bernhard came from SS Major Bernhard Krüger, after whom the mission was named. Krüger, head of a forgery unit in the Reich Security Main Office, was tasked with creating counterfeit British currency of such high quality that it would pass undetected even under close scrutiny.

The plan had two main phases:

- **Mass Production of Banknotes:** The Nazis aimed to produce tens of millions of counterfeit British pounds, ranging from £5 to £50 denominations.

- **Distribution:** The forged notes would be dropped over Britain via Luftwaffe aircraft, dispersed by Nazi agents, or used in international trade to undermine the pound's credibility.

Execution

The Nazis began assembling a team of highly skilled craftsmen, including forgers, artists, typographers, and engravers. Many of these individuals were Jewish prisoners from concentration camps, chosen for their expertise in relevant trades. The operation was set up at Sachsenhausen concentration camp, where a dedicated workshop was established for the counterfeiting efforts.

A British banknote created by the prisoners of Sachsenhausen concentration camp

Prisoners worked under harrowing conditions, knowing that failure or sabotage could result in their execution. Despite this, the team produced counterfeit notes of extraordinary quality. The fake currency was so convincing that even experts found it difficult to distinguish from genuine notes.

Production and Testing

The team produced approximately £134 million in forged notes, equivalent to over £6 billion in today's value. The counterfeit notes passed rigorous testing, including validation by German banks and international markets. The Nazis even used the forged currency to fund covert operations and bribe officials in neutral countries.

The Outcome

While the production of counterfeit notes was successful, the distribution plan faced challenges. Dropping the notes over Britain proved logistically difficult due to Allied air superiority and the need for precise targeting. Moreover, the Nazis feared that an uncontrolled flood of counterfeit currency might backfire, causing inflation in occupied territories where the pound was also used.

As a result, much of the forged currency remained unused by the end of the war. However, the operation's scale and success in creating undetectable counterfeits made it one of the most ambitious forgery schemes in history.

Significance of Operation Bernhard

Operation Bernhard's primary goal of destabilizing the British economy was never fully realized. The forged notes did not reach Britain in significant quantities to create the intended financial collapse. However, the operation demonstrated the Nazis' resourcefulness in exploring unconventional warfare methods.

Despite its failure to undermine the British economy, Operation Bernhard provided a financial boom for the Nazis. The counterfeit notes were used to fund German intelligence operations, purchase war materials on the black market, and bribe officials in neutral countries like Switzerland and Spain.

The operation had a psychological and propaganda effect. The existence of Operation Bernhard, once revealed, underscored the Nazis' willingness to exploit any means to achieve their objectives. This revelation further cemented their image as a regime capable of extraordinary cunning and deceit.

Operation Bernhard remains a case study in economic warfare and the potential of currency manipulation as a weapon of war. It highlighted the vulnerability of financial systems to counterfeiting and prompted post-war reforms in currency security.

□□*DID YOU KNOW*

- The forged notes displayed extraordinary craftsmanship, and were so convincing that even experts at the Bank of England reportedly struggled to differentiate them from genuine currency. The Nazis went to extraordinary lengths, replicating watermarks, paper texture, and even minor printing imperfections.

- The operation relied on the forced labor of concentration camp prisoners, many of whom were Jewish. While these individuals were spared immediate execution due to their skills, they lived under constant threat of death if they failed to meet the Nazis' exacting standards.

- Many of the prisoners involved in Operation Bernhard survived the war because their skills made them valuable to the Nazis. Some later recounted their experiences, offering a rare glimpse into the operation's inner workings.

- The story of Operation Bernhard inspired numerous books and films, including the Oscar-winning movie The Counterfeiters (2007). The film vividly portrays the moral dilemmas faced by the prisoners forced to aid the Nazi war effort.

- After the war, large quantities of forged notes were discovered in lakes and rivers where the Nazis had dumped them to avoid Allied capture. Some of these counterfeit notes occasionally resurface, causing intrigue among collectors and historians.

- The success of Operation Bernhard prompted post-war changes in currency design and security measures worldwide. Innovations such as complex holograms, microprinting, and advanced watermarks were developed to deter forgery.

- Ian Fleming, the creator of James Bond, was reportedly aware of Operation Bernhard during his time in British Naval Intelligence. While Fleming's direct involvement remains speculative, the operation's daring and deception align with themes in his spy novels.

A Secret Operation Within Nazi Germany

While the Nazis orchestrated Operation Bernhard, individuals within Germany opposed to Hitler had their own covert initiatives to undermine the regime. German resistance groups, including members of the military and intelligence services, conducted secret operations to sabotage the Nazi war effort and assist the Allies.

One notable example is the Operation Valkyrie plot to assassinate Hitler in July 1944. While not directly related to Operation Bernhard, these efforts reflect the internal conflicts within Germany during the war. The bravery of those who risked their lives to oppose the regime adds another layer of complexity to the story of World War II.

Legacy of Operation Bernhard

Operation Bernhard stands as one of the most audacious and complex operations of World War II. Although it failed to achieve its primary objective of collapsing the British economy, it succeeded in producing counterfeit notes of unparalleled quality and provided significant financial resources to the Nazi war machine.

The operation was a remarkable example of economic warfare and the ingenuity of both its planners and the prisoners forced to execute it.

18. OPERATION VALKYRIE (1944): THE ATTEMPT TO END HITLER'S REIGN

Here's a German operation with a difference –an operation that didn't target the Allies, but instead was a plan to kill Hitler!

Operation Valkyrie was one of the most audacious plots of World War II, organized by a group of high-ranking German officers and civilians who sought to assassinate Adolf Hitler and overthrow the Nazi regime. This daring conspiracy culminated in the infamous July 20, 1944, bombing at the Wolf's Lair, Hitler's heavily guarded headquarters in East Prussia.

While the operation ultimately failed, its significance lay in revealing the extent of internal resistance within Germany. Approximately 200 conspirators participated in the plot, risking their lives in an attempt to change the course of history.

What Was Happening in The War at This Point

By mid-1944, the war was going poorly for Germany. Allied forces had landed in Normandy and were advancing through France, while Soviet troops were pushing westward on the Eastern Front. Within Germany, dissatisfaction with Hitler's leadership grew among military officers and civilians who recognized that his obsession with total war was leading the country toward ruin.

Objective

The primary goal of Operation Valkyrie was twofold:

- **Eliminate Hitler:** Assassinate the Führer to remove the central figure of Nazi power.

- **Seize Control of Germany:** Use the pre-existing Operation Valkyrie contingency plan, designed to suppress civil unrest, as a cover to overthrow the Nazi regime and negotiate a peace settlement with the Allies.

The plotters believed that killing Hitler was essential to dismantling the Nazi state and halting Germany's catastrophic war efforts, which had already led to immense suffering and destruction.

However, the motivations of the Valkyrie conspirators were complex. While some, like Colonel Claus von Stauffenberg, were driven by moral outrage at Nazi atrocities, others were motivated by pragmatic concerns about Germany's survival. While they wanted to kill Hitler, many of their plans were anti-democratic, hoping to replace Hitler with an authoritarian government., opposing mass participation in governance.

It's thought that the plotters' demands for peace would have included re-establishment of 1914 boundaries and no reparations. It's also thought they would have wanted recognition of the full annexation of Austria, Alsace-Lorraine and Sundetenland and parts of Poland.

Details

The Conspirators

The plot was led by Colonel Claus von Stauffenberg, a decorated war hero who had lost an eye, a hand, and two fingers in combat. Stauffenberg became the central figure in the conspiracy, as he had access to Hitler's inner circle.

Claus von Stauffenberg on the left.

Other key figures included:

- General Friedrich Olbricht: Head of the Reserve Army in Berlin and a critical organizer of the coup.

General Ludwig Beck

- General Ludwig Beck: A former Chief of Staff of the German Army, who was prepared to lead a provisional government.

- Carl Goerdeler: A former mayor of Leipzig, slated to become chancellor in the post-Hitler government.

The Plan

- **Assassination Attempt:** Stauffenberg was to carry a bomb into a meeting at the Wolf's Lair and detonate it close to Hitler.

- **Implementation of Valkyrie:** After Hitler's death, the Reserve Army would be mobilized under the pretext of securing Germany from an SS coup.

- **Seizure of Power:** The conspirators would arrest key Nazi officials, including Heinrich Himmler and Joseph Goebbels, and establish a new government.

- **Negotiation with Allies:** The new government would seek a peace settlement to end the war.

The Outcome

On July 20, 1944, Stauffenberg traveled to the Wolf's Lair with a briefcase containing two time-delay bombs. However, the plot was hindered by several critical factors:

- **Only One Bomb:** Due to time constraints, Stauffenberg armed only one bomb instead of two, reducing the explosive power.

- **Placement of the Briefcase:** During the meeting, the briefcase was placed under a heavy oak table, partially shielding Hitler from the blast.

- **Hitler's Survival:** The bomb detonated, killing four people and injuring others, but Hitler escaped with minor injuries.

Believing Hitler to be dead, Stauffenberg returned to Berlin to initiate the coup. However, news of Hitler's survival quickly spread, and the conspirators' efforts unraveled. Loyal Nazi forces suppressed the uprising, and key plotters were arrested.

Ruins of the Wolf's Lair

Significance of Operation Valkyrie

The failure of Operation Valkyrie had devastating consequences for the conspirators and their families. In the months after the coup d'état attempt, the Gestapo arrested more than 7,000 people, 4,980 of whom were executed. Around 200 conspirators were executed, including Stauffenberg who was executed on the night of the failed coup. Family members were interned, including Stauffenberg's children, nephews, parents, pregnant wife, and grandmother, and their property confiscated.

Impact on the Nazi Regime

- The plot exposed cracks within the German military and government, leading Hitler to tighten his control.

- Thousands of suspected dissidents were arrested, and trust among high-ranking officials eroded further.

□□*DID YOU KNOW*

- Hitler used the failure of Valkyrie as propaganda, portraying himself as a leader chosen by fate to survive such an attack.

- The bomb's placement under the table was altered by Colonel Heinz Brandt, who unknowingly saved Hitler's life by moving the briefcase to a less effective position.

- The name "Operation Valkyrie" came from an existing German emergency plan designed to maintain control during potential uprisings. The conspirators co-opted this plan, adapting it for their coup attempt.

- Hitler issued what was known as the Sippenhaft decree (or "Sippenhaftung"), a policy rooted in the German concept of collective familial responsibility. Under this directive, family members of individuals implicated in acts of treason, including Operation Valkyrie, were held accountable and punished, regardless of their involvement or knowledge of the plot.

- The Wolf's Lair was blown up and abandoned by Nazis on January 25, 1945, two days before the Red Army arrived. It took over ten years to clear over fifty-four thousand landmines, which surrounded Wolf's Lair.

- A co-conspirator, Colonel Henning von Tresckow had organised 5 previous attempts to kill Hitler. These included shooting Hitler during dinner, but this was aborted as it was believed Hitler wore a bullet-proof vest. He also considered poisoning Hitler, but his food was always specially prepared and tasted before Hitler ate it.

Legacy of Operation Valkyrie

Although Operation Valkyrie failed, it demonstrated that not all Germans supported Hitler's regime. The conspirators' courage inspired post-war efforts to confront Germany's Nazi past, and they are remembered as symbols of resistance against tyranny.

19. OPERATION WILLI (1940): THE PLOT TO KIDNAP A PRINCE

Even the British Royal Family was not immune to German plots!

Operation Willi was a Nazi plan devised during World War II to kidnap the Duke of Windsor, Edward VIII, who had abdicated the British throne in 1936. The Germans aimed to use him as a puppet leader in Britain after a possible Nazi victory. They believed that Edward, who had expressed pro-German sentiments, could help broker peace between Britain and Germany, and possibly even restore him to the throne.

The operation was rooted in the belief that the Duke's relationship with the Nazi regime could be exploited for propaganda purposes. The Nazis hoped that kidnapping Edward and his wife, Wallis Simpson, could create a rift between Britain and its allies. They also considered using the Duke as leverage in negotiations to secure peace with the UK.

The Duke and Duchess of Windsor (to the left of Hitler) with Hitler, October 22, 1937, during their visit to The Berghof, Hitler's country house.

This plan, however, was never carried out, largely because Edward and Wallis had already left Europe, heading to Portugal in 1940, thwarting any efforts to seize them. The plot was revealed in the Marburg Files, a collection of documents recovered after the war, which detailed Nazi communications with the Duke. These files exposed Edward's flirtations with Nazi Germany and revealed that the Germans had considered using him as a tool for peace negotiations. Despite its failure, Operation Willi highlighted the ongoing tensions and intrigue surrounding the Duke of Windsor's relationship with the Nazis.

20. OPERATION PAPERCLIP (1945): RECRUITING THE BRAINS BEHIND NAZI GERMANY'S TECHNOLOGY

As the war approached its end, the United States was looking to the future, and how it could use the many talents of German scientists.

Operation Paperclip was a secret initiative launched by the United States in the final stages of World War II, with a clear goal: to harness the expertise of German scientists, engineers, and technicians. These individuals, many of whom had been pivotal in developing advanced technologies for the Nazi regime, were recruited to aid U.S. military and intelligence agencies. The operation aimed to secure a technological edge over the Soviet Union in what was quickly emerging as the Cold War. Key areas of focus included rocketry, aeronautics, and missile technology—fields where German innovations had outpaced much of the rest of the world.

As World War II drew to a close, it became evident that Nazi Germany had made significant technological advances. The V-2 rocket, the first long-range guided ballistic missile, and advanced jet aircraft designs were clear examples of this progress. Both the United States and the Soviet Union recognized the strategic importance of acquiring this expertise. The Soviets launched their own effort, known as Operation Osoaviakhim, to seize German scientists, materials, and blueprints.

For the United States, the stakes were high. The Cold War loomed on the horizon, and the need to prevent German scientists from falling into Soviet hands became urgent. Operation Paperclip was conceived to extract these valuable resources and bring them under American control. While initially framed as a defensive move against Soviet advances, the operation soon evolved into a full-scale effort to exploit German technological capabilities for the U.S.'s own military and scientific ambitions.

How Operation Paperclip Worked

1. Recruitment of Scientists

The U.S. military, spearheaded by the Army Ordnance Corps and the Office of

Strategic Services (OSS)—the precursor to the CIA—began identifying key German scientists. These individuals were often drawn from prominent Nazi research institutions such as Peenemünde (the V-2 rocket development site) and industrial giants like Daimler-Benz and Messerschmitt.

Group of 104 German rocket scientists in 1946, recruited by the U.S.

2. Selection Process

Many of the targeted scientists had strong ties to the Nazi regime, including membership in the Nazi Party or affiliations with organizations like the SS. Recognizing the moral and political sensitivities, U.S. officials devised a system to "sanitize" their pasts. A key component of the operation was issuing these scientists new biographies, often omitting or downplaying their involvement in Nazi activities. This practice became known as "paperclipping" because of the paperclips used to attach these sanitized dossiers to their profiles.

3. Relocation to the United States

The recruited scientists were quietly transported to the United States, often under the guise of military or intelligence missions. They were relocated to secure installations, including:

- Fort Bliss, Texas, where initial assessments and projects were conducted.

- Huntsville, Alabama, which became a major hub for rocket development and home to the U.S. Army's missile program.

- Langley, Virginia, where many were integrated into aviation research and military intelligence work.

4. Integration into American Programs

Once stateside, these scientists were embedded in critical U.S. programs, working on advanced weapons, aeronautics, and space exploration. Their contributions laid the groundwork for revolutionary advancements, including the development of intercontinental ballistic missiles (ICBMs), supersonic aircraft, and the Apollo space program.

Notable Figures in Operation Paperclip

- Wernher von Braun: The most famous recruit, von Braun had been a key figure in Germany's V-2 rocket program. In the U.S., he became a driving force behind the development of the Redstone missile and the Saturn V rocket, which powered NASA's Apollo missions to the Moon.

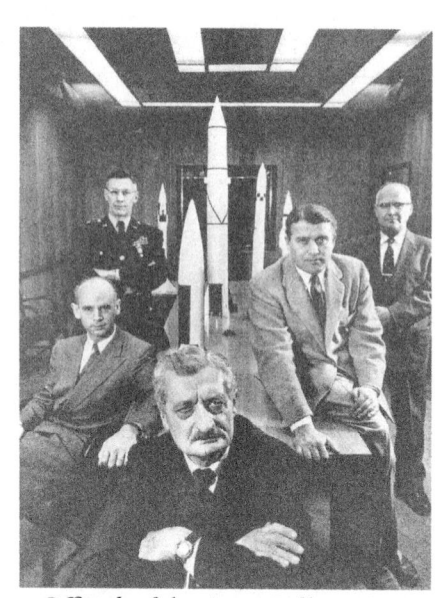

Officials of the Army Ballistic Missile Agency at Huntsville, Alabama. Includes Major General H.N. Toftoy, Commanding Officer and person responsible for Project Paperclip and Dr. Wernher von Braun. Many of the scientists later helped to design the Saturn V rocket that took the Apollo 11 astronauts to the Moon.

- Kurt Debus: An expert in rocket technology, Debus became the first director of NASA's Kennedy Space Center, overseeing the launches of early space missions and the Apollo program.

- Arthur Rudolph: A senior engineer on the V-2 rocket, Rudolph contributed to the development of the U.S. Redstone missile. However, his involvement in forced labor during the war later led to controversy, and he eventually left the U.S.

- Hubertus Strughold: Known as the "father of space medicine," Strughold conducted pioneering research on the physiological effects of space travel. However, allegations of his involvement in unethical human experiments during the Nazi era cast a shadow over his legacy.

- Hans Kammler: Although never confirmed to have participated in Operation Paperclip, Kammler was rumored to be a key figure in Nazi weapons development. His mysterious disappearance at the war's end has fueled speculation about his fate and possible U.S. collaboration.

▫▫*DID YOU KNOW*

- Many of the recruits had been deeply involved in Nazi weapons programs, including the use of forced labor from concentration camps like Mittelbau-Dora. Despite these connections, their expertise was deemed too valuable to ignore.

- The V-2 rocket, developed under von Braun's leadership, was not only a weapon of war but also the technological precursor to modern space exploration. It directly influenced the design of U.S. missiles and spacecraft.

- The U.S. government actively altered or 'Sanitized' the records of Nazi scientists to make their immigration and employment politically palatable. This effort extended to crafting entirely new identities for some individuals.

- Operation Paperclip was kept largely hidden from the public for years. Only later, through declassified documents and investigative journalism, did the full scope of the operation become known.

- In direct competition, the Soviet Union captured thousands of German scientists, including many from the same research facilities targeted by the U.S. This technological arms race was a key driver of early Cold War tensions.

- By the 1960s, several Operation Paperclip recruits had become celebrated figures in the U.S. space race, their Nazi affiliations largely forgotten or downplayed.

Controversy and Legacy

1. Ethical Questions

Operation Paperclip remains a subject of intense moral debate. Critics argue that the U.S. government prioritized technological advancement over accountability for war crimes. By recruiting individuals implicated in Nazi atrocities, the operation raised profound ethical concerns.

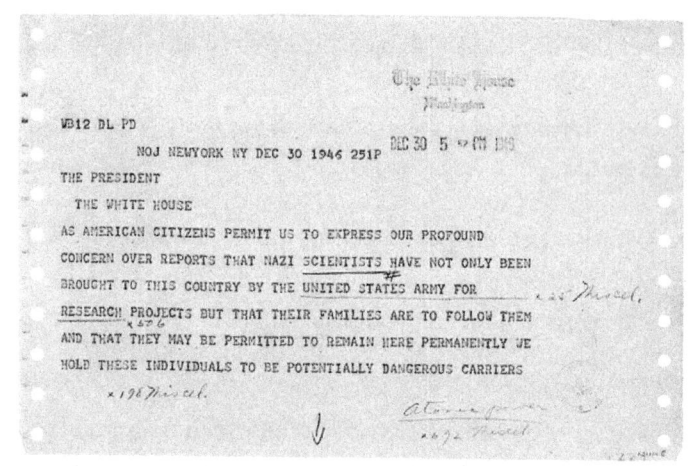

Telegram sent to Harry S. Truman opposing Operation Paperclip, endorsed by Albert Einstein, on December 30, 1946.

2. Contributions to the Cold War

The scientific contributions of Paperclip recruits helped the U.S. secure a decisive technological advantage over the Soviet Union. Their work on missiles, jet aircraft, and space technology established the foundation for the U.S.'s dominance in these fields.

3. The Question of Justice

Some of the scientists brought to the U.S. were later scrutinized for their Nazi affiliations and wartime actions. For example, Arthur Rudolph faced allegations of war crimes and was forced to renounce his U.S. citizenship in the 1980s.

4. Lasting Impact

The technological legacy of Operation Paperclip is undeniable. The recruits played a pivotal role in shaping modern aerospace engineering, military technology, and space exploration. However, the operation also serves as a reminder of the ethical compromises made in the name of national security.

Operation Paperclip's Role in the Space Race

The most visible impact of Operation Paperclip was its contribution to the U.S. space race. Wernher von Braun and his team of engineers were instrumental in developing the Saturn V rocket, which launched astronauts to the Moon during NASA's Apollo program. Without their expertise, the U.S. may have struggled to compete with the Soviet Union's early space achievements, including the launch of Sputnik and Yuri Gagarin's historic spaceflight.

Von Braun's journey from a V-2 designer for Nazi Germany to a celebrated NASA leader epitomizes the dual-edged legacy of Operation Paperclip. While his work helped achieve monumental scientific milestones, it also showed the uncomfortable compromises that defined the operation.

Operation Paperclip is one of the most controversial yet impactful initiatives of the post-World War II era, with a complex interplay of morality, politics, and science during the early Cold War. While it undeniably advanced U.S. technological capabilities and contributed to historic achievements like the Moon landing, it also forced the nation to grapple with difficult ethical questions about justice and accountability.

The operation shows the lengths nations will go to secure strategic advantages, even at the cost of compromising their principles, and is a fascinating, if troubling, chapter in the story of how World War II shaped the modern world.

21. THE MANHATTAN PROJECT: CREATING A WEAPON THAT CHANGED THE WORLD

Finally, we come to one of the most monumental, and world-changing operations of World War II - The Manhattan Project.

This was a top-secret U.S. research initiative during World War II, aimed at developing the world's first nuclear weapons. It sought to harness the power of nuclear fission to create a weapon capable of ending the war and countering the potential threat of Nazi Germany developing similar technology.

The Manhattan Project emerged from the geopolitical and scientific landscape of the late 1930s and early 1940s. In 1938, German scientists Otto Hahn and Fritz Strassmann discovered nuclear fission, igniting global interest in the potential for a powerful new weapon. Amid growing concerns about Nazi Germany's ambitions, physicists Albert Einstein and Leo Szilard wrote a letter to President Franklin D. Roosevelt in 1939, urging the U.S. to accelerate its research into atomic energy.

This led to the establishment of the Uranium Committee, an early attempt to explore nuclear technology. However, it wasn't until the United States entered World War II in December 1941 that the urgency to develop nuclear weapons intensified. In 1942, under President Roosevelt's directive, the Manhattan Project was launched as a coordinated effort to achieve this goal before Germany.

Key People and Locations

Leadership and Scientific Minds

The Manhattan Project was spearheaded by a collaboration of military leaders, scientists, and engineers:

- General Leslie R. Groves: An efficient and determined officer from the U.S. Army Corps of Engineers, Groves managed the project's logistics, including construction, security, and resource allocation.

- J. Robert Oppenheimer: Known as the "father of the atomic bomb," Oppenheimer served as the scientific director. He brought together some of the greatest minds in physics to solve the project's monumental challenges.

Dr. J. Robert Oppenheimer, atomic physicist and head of the Manhattan Project

- Other Notable Scientists: Many luminaries of the scientific world contributed, including Niels Bohr, Enrico Fermi, Edward Teller, and Leo Szilard. Many had fled Nazi-occupied Europe, adding urgency and unique expertise to the mission.

Strategic Locations

The Manhattan Project operated across several key sites:

- **Los Alamos, New Mexico:** This remote laboratory became the project's hub, where the bombs were designed and assembled.

- **Oak Ridge, Tennessee:** The site for enriching uranium using electromagnetic and gaseous diffusion techniques.

- **Hanford, Washington:** Home to the world's first large-scale nuclear reactors, which produced plutonium for the bomb.

- **University of Chicago:** The site of the first self-sustaining nuclear chain reaction, a critical milestone achieved under the direction of Enrico Fermi in 1942.

Details

The Manhattan Project focused on developing two types of bombs:

- **Uranium Bomb** – "Little Boy": This design relied on Uranium-235, a rare isotope that had to be painstakingly separated from more common Uranium-238. The bomb used a gun-type mechanism, where two sub-critical masses of uranium were brought together to trigger a nuclear chain reaction.

- **Plutonium Bomb** – "Fat Man": Using Plutonium-239 produced at Hanford, this bomb employed an implosion design. High explosives compressed a plutonium core into a supercritical state, resulting in a more sophisticated and powerful detonation.

The technical and logistical challenges were immense. Scientists had to pioneer methods for isotope separation, reactor construction, and bomb assembly—all while maintaining strict secrecy. At its peak, the project employed over 130,000 people and cost nearly $2 billion (over $25 billion today).

The Trinity Test

The project reached a critical juncture on July 16, 1945, with the Trinity Test in the New Mexico desert. This was the first detonation of a nuclear device, a plutonium bomb similar to "Fat Man." The explosion created a blinding flash, a mushroom cloud that soared 40,000 feet into the sky, and a shockwave felt over 100 miles away.

Observers were stunned by its power. Oppenheimer famously quoted the Hindu scripture Bhagavad Gita: "Now I am become Death, the destroyer of worlds."

The test's success confirmed the feasibility of nuclear weapons and set the stage for their use in warfare.

The Use of Atomic Bombs in Combat

Following the successful Trinity Test, attention turned to Japan, which remained defiant despite Germany's surrender in May 1945. To avoid a protracted invasion of the Japanese mainland, which was projected to cause millions of casualties, U.S. leaders opted to deploy the atomic bomb.

- **Hiroshima – August 6, 1945: The** uranium bomb "Little Boy" was dropped on Hiroshima, a major industrial and military hub. The explosion leveled the city, killing approximately 140,000 people by the end of the year due to the blast, firestorm, and radiation sickness.

Little Boy before being loaded into Enola Gay's (Boeing B-29 Superfortress bomber) bomb bay.

- **Nagasaki – August 9, 1945:** Three days later, the plutonium bomb "Fat Man" was dropped on Nagasaki, resulting in 70,000 deaths. The city's geography, with hills and valleys, slightly mitigated the bomb's destructive reach compared to Hiroshima.

On August 15, 1945, Japan announced its surrender, bringing World War II to an end. The atomic bombings were pivotal in forcing this decision, though their necessity remains a topic of debate.

Significance of the Manhattan Project

The Manhattan Project's success directly contributed to ending the war in the Pacific, saving countless lives by averting a drawn-out invasion of Japan. However, it also unleashed unprecedented destruction and human suffering.

The ruins of the Hiroshima Catholic Church, 1 year after the dropping of the atom bomb.

The project marked the beginning of the nuclear age, fundamentally altering global geopolitics and military strategy. The bombings of Hiroshima and Nagasaki demonstrated the catastrophic potential of nuclear weapons, shaping postwar diplomacy.

The use of atomic bombs raised profound ethical and moral dilemmas. Critics argue that Japan was on the brink of surrender and that the bombings were unnecessary, while supporters contend they were essential for ending the war swiftly.

The success of the Manhattan Project spurred a nuclear arms race between the United States and the Soviet Union, leading to decades of Cold War tension and the proliferation of increasingly powerful weapons.

The devastating power of nuclear weapons inspired international efforts to prevent their spread, including the 1968 Treaty on the Non-Proliferation of Nuclear Weapons.

▢▢*DID YOU KNOW*

- The Manhattan Project was so secret that even Vice President Harry Truman didn't learn about it until he became President in April 1945. Workers at project sites often had no idea what they were building.

- Before the Trinity Test, physicist Enrico Fermi jokingly took bets on whether the bomb's explosion would ignite the atmosphere and destroy the world. The light-hearted wager reflected the tension and uncertainty of the moment.

- Tsutomu Yamaguchi, a resident of Nagasaki, was in Hiroshima on business during the first bombing. Injured but alive, he returned to Nagasaki just in time to witness the second bombing, making him one of the few "double survivors."

Tsutomu Yamaguchi

- The project consumed 20% of the United States' electricity supply during its peak years, primarily to power the massive uranium enrichment facilities at Oak Ridge.

- The Trinity explosion fused desert sand into glass-like material, later named "Trinitite." It remains a physical reminder of humanity's first use of nuclear technology.

Legacy of the Manhattan Project

The Manhattan Project was a transformative moment in history, blending scientific innovation with military urgency. It showcased humanity's capacity for brilliance and destruction, leaving a legacy that continues to influence the modern world. While it ended World War II, it also ushered in the nuclear age, with its promise of energy and its peril of annihilation.

As nuclear weapons remain central to global security debates, the Manhattan Project serves as a stark reminder of their devastating power and the ethical responsibility that comes with wielding it. The world forever changed on that July morning in 1945, as humanity stepped into an atomic future that continues to shape our destiny.

THE LEGACY OF COURAGE AND INNOVATION

As we close the book on these 21 extraordinary operations of World War II, we reflect on a hidden war fought in the shadows. From the strategic genius of Operation Fortitude, which masterfully deceived the German High Command, to the bold sabotage of Operation Gunnerside, which crippled the Nazi atomic program, and the daring skill of the Dambusters Raid, which shattered German industrial infrastructure, these missions were a testament to human ingenuity, courage, and determination.

The people who carried out these operations - spies, scientists, commandos, and ordinary citizens - embodied the true spirit of heroism. Many of them risked their lives knowing full well they might not return, driven by an unyielding belief in freedom and the hope for a better world. Their bravery often came at a great personal cost, yet their sacrifices shaped the course of history and hastened the defeat of tyranny.

A New Kind of Warfare

These secret operations also marked the emergence of a new form of warfare - one where intelligence, deception, and precision strikes often proved as decisive as armies on the battlefield. Codebreakers like those at Bletchley Park turned cryptography into a weapon, spies infiltrated enemy lines with unmatched daring, and special operations forces redefined what was possible in military strategy. This blending of strategy, science, and subterfuge would go on to shape modern warfare, leaving a legacy that extended far beyond 1945.

Lasting Legacy

These missions left a profound legacy. They helped establish the framework for intelligence agencies like the CIA, MI6, and others around the world. Their successes highlighted the value of covert operations and collaboration between nations, setting the stage for the intelligence-sharing networks we see today. The innovations in technology and tactics have influenced modern military and counterintelligence efforts, while the resilience of those who fought serves as a timeless inspiration.

The hidden war of World War II was fought by ordinary people doing extraordinary things - they were trailblazers in a new era of warfare, showing that cleverness, determination, and courage can triumph even against overwhelming odds.

Their stories live on as a beacon of hope, a lesson in ingenuity, and a reminder of the sacrifices made for the freedoms we enjoy today. They remind us that even in the darkest of times, courage and creativity can change the world.

Thank you for reading!

If you enjoyed this book, I would be grateful if you could share your thoughts in a review on Amazon. Thank you!

ABOUT THE AUTHOR

James is a military and history expert, developing an early interest in military history from stories told by his grandfathers, one of whom was a POW spending 4 years in a camp in Poland, and even his great-grandfather, who fought at the Somme.

Whether writing about WW2, Greek Mythology, Roman Emperors or Alexander the Great, James hopes to spark a healthy curiosity and love for history in today's young people.

When not working or spending time with his wife and children, James can be found walking his two beautiful black labradors in the local countryside, pondering ideas for his next book.

See more at: james-burrows.com

Printed in Great Britain
by Amazon